Better Homes and Gardens®

PAINTED CRAFTS

BETTER HOMES AND GARDENS® BOOKS

Editor: Gerald M. Knox
Art Director: Ernest Shelton
Managing Editor: David A. Kirchner
Project Editors: James D. Blume, Marsha Jahns
Project Managers: Liz Anderson,
    Jennifer Speer Ramundt, Angela K. Renkoski

Crafts Editor: Sara Jane Treinen
Senior Crafts Editors: Beverly Rivers,
    Patricia M. Wilens
Associate Crafts Editor: Nancy Reames

Associate Art Directors: Neoma Thomas,
    Linda Ford Vermie, Randall Yontz
Assistant Art Directors: Lynda Haupert,
    Harijs Priekulis, Tom Wegner
Graphic Designers: Mary Schlueter Bendgen,
    Michael Burns, Brenda Lesch
Art Production: Director, John Berg;
    Associate, Joe Heuer;
    Office Manager, Michaela Lester

President, Book Group: Jeramy Lanigan
Vice President, Retail Marketing: Jamie L. Martin
Vice President, Administrative Services: Rick Rundall

BETTER HOMES AND GARDENS® MAGAZINE
President, Magazine Group: James A. Autry
Editorial Director: Doris Eby

MEREDITH CORPORATION OFFICERS
Chairman of the Executive Committee: E. T. Meredith III
Chairman of the Board: Robert A. Burnett
President: Jack D. Rehm

Painted Crafts
Editor: Sara Jane Treinen
Photography Editor: Beverly Rivers
Contributing Editors: Ciba Vaughan, Barbara Smith
Editorial Project Manager: Jennifer Speer Ramundt
Graphic Designer: Lynda Haupert
Electronic Text Processor: Paula Forest

Cover project: See page 54.

*P*ainting is both the most practical and the
most poetic of crafts. Practical because
with only modest skills and minimal equip-
ment (brushes and paints), even a novice
can achieve spectacular results. The poetry of
it all lies in the choices made: colors, patterns,
finishes. In Painted Crafts, *you'll find an
exciting array of materials and techniques to
explore, and a tempting variety of projects
to choose from—projects designed to delight
any paint crafter, from a preschooler to a
budding Picasso.*

CONTENTS

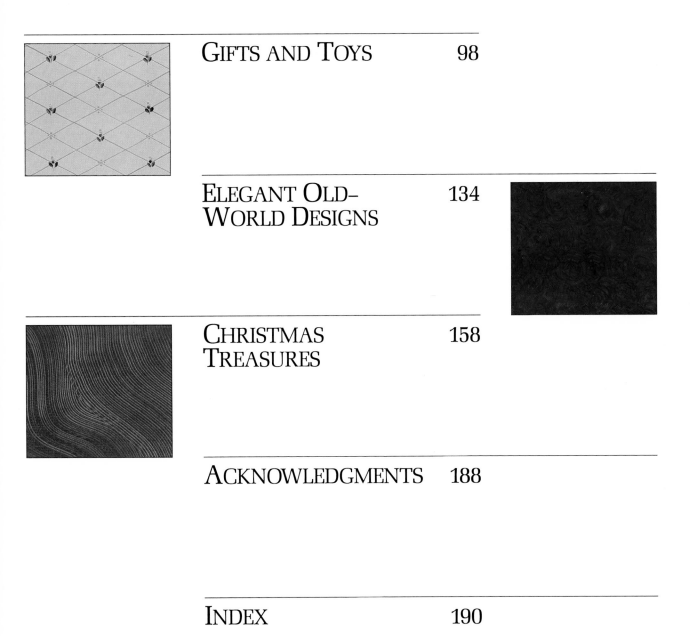

PAINTERS AT WORK

A DRAMA OF COLOR

"Painters and poets," as the Roman poet Horace once said, "have always had an equal license in bold invention." In this chapter you'll meet half a dozen painters who prove his point—six poets of the brush whose splendidly bold inventions inspire novice and expert alike.

PAINTERS AT WORK

For artist-come-lately Peg Miller, what once was just a hobby is now a full-blown career. Her exuberant, one-of-a-kind creations can be found in galleries and private collections nationwide.

Peg, who had no formal training in this area, painted her first patchwork designs in the 1960s—a spur-of-the-moment solution to problem floors at the family's summer cottage. Next came a quilt painted on plywood, on a chair, and on anything else she could find.

Below, Peg and her husband, Roy, show off some of her larger pieces in the back yard of their Spring Green, Wisconsin, home.

Peg's process is simple: Each piece is scrubbed clean with trisodium phosphate, rubbed smooth with steel wool or sandpaper, and then treated to a coat of primer and two coats of latex paint. Next, Peg draws her designs with a charcoal pencil, fills them in with latex or acrylic paints, and finally, seals them with polyurethane.

Says Peg, "I just want each of my pieces to bring a spark of joy when you see it!"

John Habercam, an artist and high school art teacher, reveals his passion for the traditional art of stenciling with a design in every room of the house which he shares with his wife Ottilie and daughters Aleigh and Courtney.

When he first started stenciling, John used purchased patterns almost exclusively. Now, most of the light and airy motifs he favors are his original designs. Notice the bouquet-and-scroll pattern, *above left,* which he adapted from the painted headboard of Aleigh's antique bed. The walls of Courtney's room, *opposite,* are abloom with stenciled tulips, per her request.

To create the doorway frame, *left,* John cut an 8-foot-long stencil of his design so he could avoid having to move the stencil again and again.

PAINTERS AT WORK

F ive years ago, painter Marie Colette sailed from France to Philadelphia with a cargo of antique Alsatian armoires. Today, she divides her time between her new American home and her native country, where she continues to scout for regional farmhouse furniture to restore and embellish in her Philadelphia basement studio.

The traditions that inspire Marie's artistry date from the early 1700s. In villages throughout western France, furniture known as "le mobilier polychrome" (multi-colored furniture) was handcrafted and painted by local artisans. Made by rural people for rural homes, most of this furniture was delightfully naive in nature.

Today, her beautiful reinterpretations of that folk art custom combine traditional patterns, techniques, and motifs with her own stylistic innovations. For example, the stylized graining on the two-panel commode, *above right,* is typical of furniture painted in Alsace two centuries ago, but the black background on the commode, *center right,* is an entirely contemporary style.

The trunk, *below right,* displays Marie's personal pictorial style in lovely, muted colors. A collection of chests and armoires, *opposite,* display the full range of this talented young woman's naive style.

PAINTERS AT WORK

As a modern-day itinerant limner (an antique term meaning "one who takes likenesses"), Debra Darnall travels the countryside painting walls, mantels, floors, and fireboards in the simplistic style of nineteenth-century muralist Rufus Porter. While the majority of Porter's work is on the eastern seaboard, most of Darnall's is in Ohio. Yet, many of her murals feature themes akin to Porter's: local scenes from the past, early buildings, landscapes, and harbors.

At *left,* the artist enjoys her painting of a ship, a sample of her work she displays at shows. *Below,* Debra brought "the outdoors in" to one client's home with this forest mural. *Opposite,* the limnist's monochromatic mural graces the stairway of her mother's home.

PAINTERS AT WORK

Pennsylvania artist and entrepreneur Ivan Barnett began by painting furniture that most people would classify as castoffs. It didn't matter what the style of a particular piece was, he wanted to change its character through color and decoration.

Today he commissions pieces of unfinished furniture from local artists. These versatile bench tables, *opposite,* are representative of Ivan's desire to combine style and function. "My furniture concepts are very close to the original influences of true folk art: they put a strong emphasis on the beauty and design of utilitarian objects."

However, it's more than practicality that makes the chair, *right,* important to Ivan. It was a family piece but he didn't like the finish. Now the newly painted chair, plus a small stool constructed from scrap lumber, fills one corner of the artist's studio. This brilliant palette of colors, with the nailed-on metal cutouts decorating the stool and the folk art frame that sits on it, are Barnett trademarks. His folk art furniture and imaginative accessories now are sold in galleries nationwide.

PAINTERS AT WORK

Using basswood, a jigsaw, and acrylic paints the way some crafters use fabric, scissors, and a needle and thread, artist Lillian Renko Bledow layers intricate cutouts into appliqué figures of delicate beauty. Much of that beauty comes from her attention to detail. Even the backs of her figures are as detailed as the fronts, enhancing the sculptural quality of each design.

For the angel, *opposite,* layers are cut out, painted, then glued together. The seated doll at her side is assembled with dowels to allow for movement.

Below are three of Lillian's many seasonal designs—St. Nicholas, a rocking horse, and a delicate summer wreath. She makes these figures professionally, but encourages novices to try their hands at similar designs.

DECORATIVE PAINTING AT HOME

◆

TO FILL YOUR HEART WITH SMILES

There's no place like home to showcase your skills. Here's an assortment of pretty ways to pattern your walls, embellish your floors, and accessorize your own cozy nest with hand-painted delights.

DECORATIVE PAINTING AT HOME

Antiquing with a splash of rubbed-in color is one easy way to add a timeworn touch to a too-new paint job. Secondhand pieces like the raised-back chair, *below,* as well as the grooved paneling, also *below,* can be finished in this way to blend more comfortably with older furnishings.

To antique a chair, shelf, or other item, first slather the piece with a coat of light-colored, oil-base paint. When this first coat is dry, brush on a second coat of paint that has been tinted with a dash of contrasting color. Immediately wipe away this second coat with a clean rag, then rub the painted piece with a second clean rag to remove all vestiges of color from the raised surfaces. Bright channels of color will remain in the grooves and crevices of the incised design.

Distressing is another quick and easy technique for adding a patina of age to a freshly painted finish. The hanging cupboard on the wall, *opposite,* began as an unfinished purchased piece. After receiving a coat of blue latex paint, the cupboard was lightly sanded in strategic spots to "distress" the surface, imitating the natural wear and tear of age. A light glaze of raw umber paint, thinned with oil, further evokes the timeworn look we all love so well.

The no-sew quilt on the wall behind the cupboard is a nine-patch design stamped on the wall with cut-to-size squares of heavy-duty boat and deck sponge. The sponge squares are dipped in assorted colors of paint, squeezed almost dry, then positioned and stamped directly on the wall, which has been prepared with a coat of background color. The same technique works well on any flat prepared surface, including the little side table, *opposite.*

How-to instructions for these projects begin on page 29.

DECORATIVE PAINTING AT HOME

Fresh paint, applied in a bright mix of colors and sprightly patterns, is one sure way to make almost anything old look new again. The show-stopping floor at *right* once was deemed beyond salvation. But a splashy new wall-to-wall "carpet" in a bold pattern of painted squares and stenciled heart motifs turned that plain floor into a fabulous focal point for the entire room.

To create this distinctive floor, first paint the surface with several coats of capri blue and allow it to dry. Then carefully mark off the surface in a pattern of diagonal squares. Next paint on contrasting blocks of luscious hydrangea and allow it to dry.

Finally, stencil ginger peachy hearts with bittersweet tendrils in one corner of each hydrangea square, and then treat the entire floor to several coats of polyurethane.

To complete the room's special look, paint unfinished furniture, trim, woodwork, and assorted accessories in a palette picked up from the floor pattern (see the shelf, *above,* and the settee and woodwork, *right*). It's a great way to mix and match up pieces of cast-off furniture that otherwise might not work together in the same room.

24

DECORATIVE PAINTING AT HOME

For problem walls and floors, simple solutions are often the best. A well-worn plank floor, *opposite*, is rejuvenated with a painted checkerboard pattern of bold yellow and white squares. Laid out with a yardstick and strips of masking tape, this pattern can be tailored to suit any size room.

For the patterned walls, *opposite*, simply stipple paint through a purchased stencil pattern around the borders of the room. Use a light touch with the brush to achieve a slightly faded, old-fashioned look.

For the two-tone sponged look, *above*, use one color of oil-base paint for the background, and a contrasting color for the sponged-on pattern. This application is particularly effective in combination with painted trim and a complementary wallpaper, as illustrated here.

Fantasy spatter-painted frames like those *above* are easy and inexpensive to make. Choose a plain purchased frame of appropriate size and paint it with a neutral base color. Then, using an old toothbrush and a selection of artist's acrylics, spatter the frame with two or three colors that echo those of the picture to be framed. Taupe, rose, and brown were used to accent these off-white frames, but any combination of colors would work as well.

IMAGINATIVE TIPS AND IDEAS FOR PAINTING YOUR WALLS

Walls can—indeed should—do a lot more than just hold up the ceiling. They are the largest expanse of decorative surface you have to work with, and they set the stage for the rest of your furnishings. In fact, what you do with your walls can make up for the architectural shortcomings that may exist in your rooms. Whatever the mood you want to achieve, you can find a number of possibilities in a can of paint.

Color is one of the most powerful forces in the visual world. Simply by using a single *light* paint color, you can move walls back, raise or lower ceilings, stretch floor space, and entirely reshape your room's environment. When you paint the walls, ceiling, and woodwork of a small room with one light color, you become less conscious of the wall space and the room "feels" more expansive.

Color also allows you to change a room's dimensions. Begin by sizing up your room's space. If its dimensions aren't pleasing, you can reshape your room by emphasizing or eliminating contrasts. Use bold, bright, or dark colors selectively to draw in a wall or lower a ceiling. For example, make a long and narrow room appear "squarer" by painting the ceiling and longer walls with a light neutral color (to visually push the walls out) and the opposite walls a contrasting bright color (to pull the end walls in).

Use color and paint to dramatize a room's architectural features. If you want to accent the charm of angles, woodwork, or windows, showcase them deliberately with contrasts. Evaluate your room's assets, then play them up (or down). Irregular walls and low ceilings, for example, can be absolutely charming when you select the correct contrasts.

If you want to emphasize the interesting oddities in a small room, use vertical patterns (either wallpaper or comb painting) to visually lift the ceiling and make the walls appear taller. Then paint the angles, ceiling, and woodwork with light colors to open up these spaces. It's best to keep the number of colors and patterns to a minimum when working in a confined space.

If you want to achieve the opposite effect and minimize architectural oddities, avoid contrasts completely and paint nooks, crannies, and radiators the same color as the walls and ceiling.

Textured walls, whether slick or dull, smooth or rough, give a room surface appeal and decorative interest. Contrasting textures engage your tactile sense as well as your visual sense. Playing strong textures against subtle ones creates variety in rooms dominated by one color or by a neutral color scheme. In fact, it enriches any decor. Another advantage of textured

wall treatments is that they can mask a multitude of minor surface blemishes. This can be especially helpful in an older house.

For a stuccolike finish, use a premixed wall coating that is applied with a putty knife, spread with a trowel, and then textured with any number of imaginative items. The coating stays pliant long enough for you to work it into the desired pattern and correct any mistakes. Experiment with combing, stippling with crushed paper towels, or even making designs with your fingertips to achieve interesting and varied textures.

A bold or subtle grid painted on a wall or ceiling makes a strong personal statement and enlivens a bland space. Use this approach if you want to accent architectural details or to divert attention from unwanted features. Work out your design to scale on graph paper using felt-tip markers to simulate the colors. Once you are satisfied with the design, draw the design onto the wall or ceiling. You can paint single lines using masking tape or, if you'd like more than one narrow parallel line, use the tape that's designed for painting stripes on cars. This tape is an inch wide and is scored with strips that can be pulled away to expose areas you want to paint.

Stenciled Phrase On Washed Walls

Shown on page 21.

MATERIALS
For the color wash
Off-white latex semigloss paint
(base coat)
Brush or roller (to apply base coat)
Two 4-inch-wide brushes (to apply
color wash)
Raw sienna acrylic paint
Paint tray (for color wash)
Clear mat polyurethane varnish
(optional)

For the stenciling
4-inch-high letter stencils or
acetate stencil material
Oil-base wax crayon or stencil
paint
Stencil brush
Crafts knife
Masking tape; level

INSTRUCTIONS
PREPARATION: Scrub and clean
walls. Lightly sand all rough surfaces and fill cracks, dents, and
holes with filler.

FOR THE BASE COAT: Roll or
brush a coat of off-white semigloss
paint onto the wall; let paint dry
overnight.

FOR THE WASH MIXTURE: First,
calculate the square footage of your
room. Then mix the following ingre-
dients to make the glazing solution
for the washing of your walls: To
cover an 8x12-foot wall, combine
½ cup of off-white semigloss paint,
⅛ teaspoon of raw sienna acrylic
paint, and ½ cup of water; mix well.
Before glazing the wall, test the
glaze mixture on a large piece of
scrap wood painted with the base
coat. Allow the base coat on the test
board to dry; then brush on the
glaze. Once the glaze on the board is
dry, determine if the color is too
dark, too light, or too thick.
If the wash is too dark, lighten it
with paint. If the wash is too light,
add a small amount of raw sienna. If
the wash mixture is too thick, thin

with water. Repeat the test on the
board until satisfactory results are
achieved.
It is important to prepare the test
board. If the wash is too dark,
opaque, or thick, it will create a
stormy effect rather than a gently
washed appearance on your wall.
Once you are satisfied with the
wash on your test board, apply the
glaze to your wall, moving the brush
in all directions to prevent the wash
from running or trickling down the
wall. The brush pattern should be
irregular but it should glaze over every inch of the base coat. Avoid
overbrushing.
Brush out any obvious edges. If
necessary, use the second brush
(dry) to mop up trickles. Let the wall
dry overnight before applying the
stenciled letters.

FOR THE STENCILING: To make
the 4-inch-high letters, draw your
own letters onto separate sheets of
lined or graph paper. Draw around
the letters to make them ½ inch
wide. Cut a stencil pattern for each
letter from acetate, allowing a 1-
inch border around each letter.
On the wall, use a level and a
pencil to draw two parallel lines 4
inches apart for placement of the
phrase. Tape your paper letter patterns to the wall between the lines
to establish their placements and to
position the phrase. Draw around
the letters.
Remove the letters. Stencil the
phrase onto the wall following the
manufacturer's instructions on the
wax crayon or stencil paint.
If you want to be able to wash
(clean) the walls, varnish them with
the polyurethane varnish.

Stucco Walls

Shown on page 22.

MATERIALS
Ready-mixed drywall compound
Cement trowel; putty knife
Off-white oil-base semigloss paint
(or desired color)

INSTRUCTIONS
Scrub and clean walls. It is not necessary to fix small cracks, dents,
and holes because the stucco compound will repair these areas. If
wall areas are raised, you may want
to sand them off prior to applying
the drywall compound.
Prepare the drywall compound
for application following the manufacturer's instructions. Working
from top to bottom on a 3-foot-wide
area of the wall, use the trowel and
putty knife to apply a ⅛- to ¼-inch
layer of the compound.
After the area is covered, use the
trowel to lay the compound flat
against the wall. At the same time,
pull the compound away with the
trowel to create a rough texture. Repeat the smoothing and pulling ac-
tion until the surface is irregularly
roughened. Avoid a regular, con-
trived texture. Clean the trowel.
Next use side-to-side and up-and-
down motions to broadly sweep the
trowel across the roughened areas,
creating high and low textures.
Continue this procedure in the
next 3-foot section, blending the previously worked area into the new
one. Work quickly to blend the areas before the compound dries. Let
the compound dry for two days.
Paint the wall with the off-white
paint or the desired color.
To add an aged look, prepare an
antiquing glaze following the instructions for the Antiqued Paneling
on page 30. Apply a thin coat of the
glaze to the painted stucco.

Color-Rubbed Chair

Shown on page 22.

MATERIALS
White oil-base paint
Artist's red oil color or desired
color for rubbing
Pressed-back chair or other
desired piece of furniture
Paint thinner; empty can
2-inch-wide brush
Fine-grit sandpaper
Two soft, clean, absorbent cloths
Mat finish varnish (optional)
continued

INSTRUCTIONS

Color rubbings bring out the interesting textural details in sculptural wood pieces and, like antiquing, add imaginative coloring to flat surfaces. To begin, scrape off any loose particles of old varnish or paint on the furniture piece and sand all rough edges smooth. Paint the chair with two thin coats of white oil-base paint, allowing each coat to dry thoroughly.

In the can, mix ½ cup of white paint to 2 tablespoons of paint thinner. Add 3 tablespoons of the artist's red oil color and stir the paints to make an even color mixture. The color mixture should be much more intense than the desired finished color. This is necessary because the color will be much more pale once it is rubbed off the piece.

Working in small sections at a time, brush the paint mixture onto the chair. Wipe away the paint with one cloth, soaking up most of the paint. With the second cloth, rub the surface with circular motions to remove almost all of the color. As you rub, the bright color will remain in the grooves of the chair's sculptured details.

When the piece is completely dry, apply two coats of varnish.

Antiqued Paneling
Shown on page 22.

MATERIALS
Off-white oil-base semigloss paint
 (or desired color)
Brush or roller to apply base coat
Oil-base varnish
Paint thinner
Raw umber artist's oil paint
Japan drier (available at art supply
 stores)
Empty can for mixing glaze
2-inch-wide brush
Lint-free rags

INSTRUCTIONS
Paint the paneled or molding surface with the off-white paint; let dry.

In the can, mix an antiquing glaze that consists of 1¼ cups varnish, ½ cup Japan drier, and ¼ cup paint

SPONGE-STAMPED WALL

1¾"

1¾"

thinner. One cup of glaze will cover approximately 20 square feet. Mix 1 tablespoon of raw umber paint into the glaze. You can add more raw umber if you wish to achieve a darker antiquing color. Before you begin it is best to practice the antiquing on an off-white painted scrap of wood to determine the color you desire.

Working over an area that is approximately 12 square feet, brush the glaze over the painted paneling with the 2-inch-wide brush. Brush out any runs and trickles as the glaze begins to set.

Let the glaze set for approximately 10 minutes.

Rub the glazed surface with the rag, wiping away much of the glaze and allowing the color to remain in the grooves. Continue to add the glaze to the remaining portions of the paneling, stroking out the glaze in overlapping areas.

Apply a coat of varnish to the antiqued surface.

Sponge-Stamped Wall

Shown on page 23.

MATERIALS

Accent Country Colors (2-fluid-ounce jars): One jar *each* of adobe wash (2311), pink blossom (2409), off-white (2428), and April showers (2510) to cover a 6x8-foot wall
Medium-dark rusty-rose latex paint
Boat and deck sponge
Plastic plate (palette)
Paper towels
18-inch-long metal woodworker's level
Pencil; serrated knife

INSTRUCTIONS

Note: The directions, *right,* will fit evenly on a 6x8-foot wall. Make adjustments, as desired, for the overall pattern on your wall, or paint a portion of the pattern on the wall as a painted quilt. Each block of the pattern (six stamps by six stamps) is about 25½ inches square.

Carefully read the directions and graph out the pattern for your wall before you begin to paint.

PREPARATION: Since the sponge is easier to cut when stiff, wash the new sponge in soapy water, rinse, and allow to dry until firm. When dry, cut a 2½-inch square stamp from the sponge with the serrated knife.

Clean, then paint wall with the rusty-rose paint; let dry. When paint is dry, mark a vertical line 1¾ inches in from the corner of the wall (if you want the design to begin at the corner). Use the level as a straight-edge as well as for a plumb line.

STAMPING THE WALL: *Note:* Because the sponge is flexible when wet, the stampings tend to expand slightly and exact measurements are difficult to determine ahead of time. The pattern lines are best established as you paint.

Squeeze a few tablespoons of adobe wash paint on the plastic plate and lightly dampen the sponge; at the same time spread the paint around the plate surface with the sponge, flattening the paint until it makes a sticking sound. Lift the sponge from the plate, and practice stamping on paper until you achieve a lightly textured stamp.

Working along the marked vertical line, stamp the sponge on the wall at the top corner making sure the two opposite corners lie on the line. Continue stamping down the vertical line. Notice the white line of squares near the left in the photo on page 23.

All of the next stampings will work from this line. Referring to the drawing, *opposite,* count down six stamps from the top. At the center of the sixth stamp, draw a horizontal line across the wall with the level. Count down another six stamps and mark another horizontal line. Continue drawing horizontal lines every sixth stamp until you reach the bottom of the wall (or the end of the planned area).

Stamp the horizontal lines with the adobe wash paint, replenishing the paint as needed.

On one of the horizontal lines of stamps, count six stamps to the right of the first vertical line. At the center tip of this stamp, use the level to mark a vertical line from the top to the bottom of the wall. Count another six stamps to the right and mark another vertical line. Continue to draw vertical lines until you reach the opposite corner of the wall (or the end of your planned area).

Stamp the vertical lines with adobe wash paint. You now have a grid pattern established on your wall.

Clean the plate with water and put a few tablespoons of April showers paint on it. Inside each square of the adobe wash squares, stamp April showers squares. When these squares are all stamped, stamp off-white squares inside the April showers squares. Complete the patchwork design by stamping pink blossom squares inside the off-white squares. The center five rusty-rose squares of each patchwork unit remain unstamped.

Distressed Hanging Cupboard

Shown on page 23.

MATERIALS

Blue latex paint
Fine, medium-, and heavyweight sandpapers
Raw umber oil-base artist's paint
Paint thinner
2-inch-wide brush
Empty tuna can (for mixing antiquing glaze)
Soft, clean, absorbent cloth
Varnish; sanding sealer

INSTRUCTIONS

Note: Distressing wood, as described on page 33, can be applied to any wood surface. The technique works best on wood that has been stripped and sanded. Nicks and dents need not be filled. We used blue paint, but you can use any base coat color that will complement your decorating scheme. Just substitute your color for the blue paint in these directions.

continued

PREPARING AND FINISHING PAINTED FLOORS

Painted or stenciled floors are a wonderful and economical way to bring color and design into any room. Whether you choose to apply a color wash, stencil a border pattern, or paint splendid and intricate designs that simulate marbling or parquet, floor paintings are both practical and imaginative. You can design complex floor paintings that will serve as the main focus of a room with simple furnishings or neutral walls and fabrics, or you can coordinate a more simple painting to complement upholstery fabrics and wallpaper designs.

However you decide to use color on your floors, there are some necessary steps you must take to ensure satisfactory results and durability.

Once you have selected the design and colors for your floor, it is best to begin the painting process when windows can be open and the air is dry. Clear the room of all furniture.

The best results are achieved when paint is applied to a clean, freshly sanded floor where the wood blemishes have been sanded out, splinters and indentations have been removed, the floor is level, and any substantial holes have been filled. (If you're planning to finish your floors with polyurethane varnish, then fill holes with a polyurethane filler.)

You can do the sanding yourself (rent a power sander from a lumber or hardware store) or have it done professionally. When the sanding is completed, vacuum the floor, scrub it with a mixture of water and a little bleach, let it dry, and then thoroughly wipe it with a tack cloth.

Purchase a tack cloth at any paint supply store or make your own. To do it yourself, dip an old, clean, 12-inch square cloth in warm water and wring out. Then dip it into mineral spirits and wring out again. Pour 3 or 4 teaspoons of varnish onto the cloth and with your hands, work the varnish into the cloth so it is evenly distributed. Always store the cloth in an airtight container when not in use. If the cloth dries out, repeat the process.

The floor paintings on pages 25 and 26 are relatively simple and easy to accomplish. Detailed instructions for the actual paintings follow in this chapter.

Your painted finishes will withstand the normal household wear and tear only if you protect them with several coats of varnish.

You even can touch them up with a refresher coat every other year, if desired.

Polyurethane varnish is easy to apply. It is tough, both stain- and heat-resistant, and is available in several gloss finishes—mat, semigloss, or gloss. Your choice should depend on the amount of shine you desire. Use the tack cloth to clean up any dust particles before you begin to wipe on the varnish. To apply the varnish, first wipe the loaded varnish brush *across* the grain of a small area; then wipe it even *with* the grain. Continue this double stroking technique with the varnish until the floor is completely covered. Allow the varnish to dry overnight (sometimes longer, depending on the humidity).

With fine sandpaper, sand the floor lightly before applying the second coat. For this step, you can use a hand-held power sander or wrap the paper around a block of wood and sand by hand. Continue to apply coats of varnish—up to five coats—to ensure the best durability. You can even wax the floor after varnishing is complete to improve its look. Just make sure you remove the wax before applying any touch-up varnish coats.

First apply a coat of sanding sealer to the stripped wood surfaces; let dry. Smooth the raised wood with fine sandpaper. Then paint it with the blue latex paint or another latex paint color of your choice.

With heavyweight sandpaper, distress the surface by sanding it, following the direction of the wood grain. Sand unevenly and in places that logically would be worn, scratching the surface.

With medium-weight sandpaper, wear down the edges of the piece until the raw varnished wood beneath clearly shows through. Concentrate on areas that naturally would wear with use and age.

In the mixing can, use the brush to mix a thin (water consistency) antiquing glaze of raw umber and paint thinner. Mix one dab of paint to about ⅓ cup of paint thinner.

Brush glaze over entire piece. Use the cloth to rub away the glaze, leaving just a hint of the raw umber color on the surface. Occasionally stroke through the glaze to create a wood grain appearance.

Apply two coats of varnish to protect the surface.

Painted and Stenciled Floor

Shown on pages 24 and 25.

MATERIALS

Sophir Morris latex paints in the following colors: Capri blue (Q12-2P), hydrangea (Q14-42T), bittersweet (Q7-54D), and ginger peachy (Q2-53P)
Wood primer; sanding sealer
Mat finish polyurethane varnish
Two 3- to 4-inch-wide brushes
Small brush for touch-ups
Yardstick; cardboard
Painter's tape or ½-inch-wide masking tape
Plastic acetate for stencil
Crafts knife; stencil brush
Two flat pans for stencil paints
Steel wool
Sandpaper
Tack cloth
Paint thinner

INSTRUCTIONS

Refer to the tips, *opposite,* to prepare the floor for painting. On our floor, we first cleaned the floor by scrubbing it with steel wool dipped in paint thinner. Then we lightly hand-sanded following the wood grain and cleaned it again with floor cleaner. When the floor was dry, we wiped it with a tack cloth.

If you are painting a floor that is newly sanded, first seal, then prime the floor. If you are working on a floor that already is varnished and waxed, it is important to remove the wax and apply a sanding sealer before you begin painting. Prime the floor; let dry. Then paint the entire floor with two coats of capri blue, allowing paint to dry completely between coats.

LAYING OUT THE PATTERN: The checkerboard design on pages 24 and 25 is a pattern of 12-inch squares arranged in diagonal rows creating diamond shapes. To begin, mark center of each wall at the baseboard. Mark the center of the room by drawing two perpendicular lines across the center of the floor.

Cut a 12-inch square from the cardboard. Center the square diagonally over the intersection of the two lines so the corners align with the drawn lines. Draw around the square. Continue to draw squares, in all four directions, over the drawn lines. After lines are covered, draw squares on the remaining floor using the existing squares as a guide until the entire floor is marked off.

continued

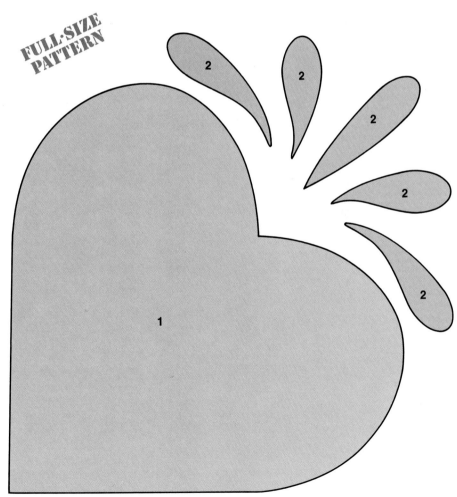

FULL·SIZE PATTERN

STENCIL PATTERN FOR PAINTED AND STENCILED FLOOR

PAINTING THE FLOOR: Draw an X in alternating squares. These squares will be painted hydrangea. Use the masking or painter's tape to outline the squares that will be painted hydrangea. Use long strips and lay the tape along the lines *inside* the blue squares. Begin painting with the hydrangea in the centers of the squares and brush the paint toward the edges so a heavy flow of paint does not seep under the edges of the masking tape. Allow the paint to dry, then paint the hydrangea squares again.

When the paint is completely dry, remove the masking tape. Use the small paintbrush to touch up the blue paint along the edges where the masking tape was removed.

STENCILING THE FLOOR: Trace the heart and leaf stencil pattern on page 33 onto the acetate; use the crafts knife to cut out the stencil.

Place small amounts of bittersweet and ginger peachy paints into the flat pans. Position the stencil pattern into one corner of one hydrangea square and stencil the heart with the ginger peachy and the leaves with the bittersweet. Referring to the photo on page 25, continue to stencil the heart design in one corner of each square. Notice how the heart motif lies in the same direction throughout. If you want to de-emphasize the direction of the heart pattern, stencil the motif in opposite corners of each square to give an overall appearance.

FINISHING: Protect the floor with two to three coats of varnish, allowing each coat to dry and lightly sanding between each coat. Apply wax to finish the floor, if desired.

If you want your floor to have an aged look, lightly sand the floor to scratch the surface before applying the varnish. Sand unevenly and in places that logically would be worn. Then use a soft cloth to apply an antiquing glazing mixture of raw umber artist's paint with paint thinner. Prepare this mixture using one dab of raw umber to about ⅓ cup of thinner. Apply the varnish and wax as directed *above*.

Yellow and White Checkerboard Floor
Shown on page 26.

MATERIALS
Yellow and white latex
  or deck paints
Mat finish polyurethane varnish
Two 3- to 4-inch-wide brushes
Small paintbrush for touch-ups
Yardstick; chalk line
½-inch-wide masking tape
Graph paper

INSTRUCTIONS
Refer to the tips on page 32 to prepare the floor for painting.

LAYING OUT THE PATTERN: The checkerboard design on page 26 is an arrangement of squares. To begin, make a scale drawing of your floor on the graph paper. Examine the size of your room and then determine the size of the squares. Keep in mind that larger squares will make the room appear larger, and smaller squares will tend to diminish the size of the room. Normally squares measure from 12 to 16 inches depending on the room size. You even can cut finished-size squares from paper and lay them on your floor to see how the arrangement fits your room.

You also might consider a border of solid color around the perimeter of the room with the painted design inside it. Whatever you decide, it is important to plan the placement of the checkerboard design so it works out evenly on your floor.

PAINTING THE FLOOR: Paint the entire floor with the white paint; let dry. Then paint the floor again with the white paint. If you decide to paint your floor with a color other than yellow or white, *always* paint the entire floor with the lighter paint color first.

When the white paint is completely dry, use the yardstick and chalk line to snap the square pattern across the room. First snap the horizontal lines equal distances apart

(the size of your squares), then snap the vertical lines perpendicular to the horizontal ones.

Use the masking tape to outline the squares on the floor. Use long strips and lay the tape along the chalk lines inside the white squares. Paint the yellow squares. It is best to begin the painting in the centers of the squares and brush the paint to the edges so a heavy flow of paint does not seep under the edges of the masking tape. Depending on the intensity of the color of yellow that you desire, you can paint a second yellow coat.

When the paint is completely dry, remove the masking tape. Use the small paintbrush to touch up white or yellow paint along the edges where the masking tape was removed. Protect the floor with two to three coats of varnish, allowing each coat to dry and lightly sanding between each coat. Apply wax to finish the floor, if desired.

Spatter-Painted Picture Frames
Shown on page 27.

MATERIALS
Off-white flat latex paint
Old newspapers
Old toothbrushes
Metal knife
Taupe, rose, and brown acrylic
  paints
Frame or other item you wish to
  spatter-paint
Paint palette with three cups
High-gloss, clear spray varnish

INSTRUCTIONS
Paint the frame with off-white latex paint; let dry.

Because spatter painting is messy, cover your work area with old newspapers or work outdoors.

Place a small amount of each acrylic paint in a palette cup and thin each to a water consistency.

Before beginning to spatter-paint the frame, practice the technique on newspapers. Try to obtain even spattering. Dip the toothbrush into the paint. Sweep the metal knife across the bristles, and let the paint spray the frame. Do not overload the brush. Spatter taupe first to make a dense covering. Clean the brush, than spatter the rose paint. Clean the brush, and spatter a small amount of brown to highlight the surface.

Acrylic paints dry quickly so you do not need to wait a long time for drying between color changes. Also, if you do not like the coloring of your spattering, wipe off the acrylic paint with a damp cloth and begin again.

When the paint is dry, spray the frame with several coats of varnish.

Sponged Wall

Shown on page 27.

MATERIALS
Medium-size sea sponge
Off-white flat oil-base paint (base coat) or another light color of your choice
Semigloss oil-base paint in darker or lighter color than base coat (for sponging)
Turpentine
Boiled linseed oil
Paint tray
Old newspapers and rags
Paint thinner for cleaning up oil-base paints
Paint roller to apply base coat

INSTRUCTIONS
Use the roller to apply the flat paint to the walls and allow the paint to completely dry.

You can do the sponging using either one of the following two methods. You can sponge the paint *onto* the wall or sponge the paint *off* the wall. Practice both methods on a piece of scrap wood to decide which one you prefer.

In both methods, first thin the semigloss paint with equal parts of linseed oil and turpentine to make a tinted transparent glazing mixture.

To sponge the paint onto the wall, use the sea sponge to apply the transparent mixture. Place about 1 cup of the mixture into the paint tray and dab the sponge into the paint without overloading it. Blot the excess paint onto newspapers and then begin the sponging onto the wall. Space the patches of color randomly on the wall, changing the position of the sponge frequently to achieve an irregular, mottled effect. Sponge quickly until the paint fades, then reload the sponge and repeat. Replenish the paint tray as needed and continue the procedure until the wall is covered.

To sponge the paint from the wall, first brush the transparent mixture onto the wall. Using the sponge, dab the wet paint to remove the paint and to create the mottling. Periodically clean the sponge with a solvent to prevent it from becoming overloaded with paint.

If you want to obtain a more colorful effect with the sponging technique, use two colors of glazing mixture. You can use either method to apply the colors, but you will have better success if you dab the colors onto the wall, creating the color contrasts as you work.

REPAIRING PLASTER WALLS AND DRYWALL

No matter what kind of walls you have, you undoubtedly will need to do some repair work before painting. Spackling hairline cracks on plaster walls is relatively easy. First widen the crack to about ⅛ inch by running a thin blade up and down the fissure. Dig out the crack about an inch past each end. Use your finger to rub the crack with spackling compound, pressing it into the opening. Force the filler in as deep as you can. You may need to repeat this after an hour or so. When the patch is dry, lightly sand and seal the patch with primer before painting.

To patch large plaster cracks, undercut the crack to make it broader underneath than on the surface. Mix a small batch of patching plaster or use premixed joint compound. If you use plaster, thoroughly wet the crack just before patching to ensure a secure bond. Pack the patching material into the crack with a putty knife or wide-blade taping knife. After 24 hours, make a second application to level off the repair. When the second coat is dry, smooth with fine sandpaper or a damp sponge. Seal with primer before painting.

To repair dents on drywall, sand the depression to roughen the surface. Pack the area with joint compound. A second coat might be needed if the patch shrinks while it is drying. Blend the patch with a light sanding or by wiping with a damp sponge. Prime, then seal or shellac the patch.

To mend split tape on drywall, use a sharp knife to gently lift the loose tape. Cut carefully at the edges, or you may pull off material from either side of the tape. Smooth the rough spots with fine sandpaper. Apply joint compound to the wall surface and position new tape. Smooth out bubbles with light, vertical knife strokes. While compound is still wet, apply a second coat. Let dry, then lightly coat again, feathering out the edges. Sponge or sand when dry to get a smooth surface.

START TO FINISH

◆

FIVE PAINTING TECHNIQUES

In this chapter are five easy painting finishes—faux marbleizing, tortoiseshell painting, comb and vinegar painting, and a crackling technique—that prove the joy and magic of paint. Turn unwanted pieces of furniture into decorating treasures and lively conversation starters.

START TO FINISH

One of the oldest and most popular of all painted finishes, marbling comes in many guises. Early examples can be found on Mycenaean pottery and plastered Roman temple columns. During the Renaissance, the French and Italians marbled ceilings, shutters, doors, and walls. During the neoclassic period, English artisans marbled small wooden tables to imitate the bronze and marble tables that recently had been unearthed in Pompeii. Marbling has continued to be used extensively throughout the last few centuries to decorate all types of woodwork and furnishings.

A whimsical approach to the technique—which captures the rich colors and patterning of marble without actually duplicating nature—is at the heart of the marbling method detailed here.

As with any of the finishes in this chapter, marbling can be applied to almost any surface but it looks particularly intriguing on curved or sculptured surfaces, such as the carved detailing on this side table, *opposite.* And because natural marble comes in a wide variety of colors, you can easily work with paint colors that complement almost any decor.

Before starting this painting process, lightly sand the piece. Apply one coat of primer, let it dry thoroughly, then lightly sand again.

Use oil-base enamel paints for the actual marble application.

1. The first step in marbleizing is to haphazardly brush on a combination of three to five colors in a small area, creating a patchwork effect. *Below,* the artist works with pink, white, gray, and a mossy green.

2. With loosely crumpled newspaper or a sponge, carefully dab the paint colors onto one another, patting the paper up and down. It is important not to smudge or smear the colors. The secret is to dab lightly to achieve a mottled effect. Don't be afraid to work fast— the more spontaneous the movement, the more realistic the marbling.

3. If you work with a sponge rather than newspaper, first apply the patchwork of colors as described in Step 1, then sponge over each area of wet color immediately.

For either technique, experiment on a scrap piece of wood before tackling a piece of furniture.

Repeat the marbling process until the entire piece is painted. Allow the paint to dry.

4. With a thin brush, add veins of color randomly across the mottled surface of the marble. Use both light and heavy strokes, as well as a combination of smooth and jagged ones, to create realistic uneven veining. To finish, apply several coats of high-gloss polyurethane, sanding between coats.

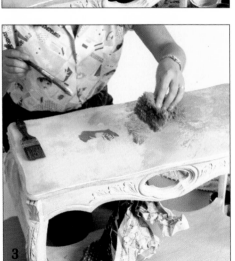

START TO FINISH

This inventive finish is one easy way to make even the newest piece of unfinished furniture—or a favorite garage sale find—look like a treasured country antique. Crackling, a new technique spawned by the current rage for old-time looks in furnishings, makes use of contemporary products (latex paints and hide glue) to imitate the effects of aging on old paint.

The finish can be created in any combination of latex colors. (A light color over a dark background is preferable. But, a dark color over a lighter background also works.) Here, a nontraditional mix of pink and white crackles as convincingly as any blend of old colonial paints.

Although crackling is not an authentic "traditional" painting technique, it creates an appealing old-fashioned finish that you'll want to try on a variety of pieces.

One tip: If you're working with a pre-painted piece of furniture there's no need to strip off the original coat of paint. Just treat the painted surface to an overall coat of liquid sander before tackling the crackling.

1. To begin, assemble the following materials: fine-grit sandpaper and sanding sealer (or white shellac); primer and off-white semigloss latex paint for the base coat; pink semigloss latex for the crackle coat; masking tape; hide glue; clear polyurethane varnish; and a 2-inch-wide nylon brush.

2. Lightly sand the raw wood, then seal with a coat of sanding sealer or white shellac to prevent wood blemishes, such as knots, from bleeding through the painted finish.

Paint the piece with primer followed by a base coat of off-white latex. When the paint is dry, use masking tape to tape off areas that are to be crackled. We began with the raised center panels on the door.

3. Mix a solution of two parts hide glue to one part water in a disposable container. Stir thoroughly. Then, using the nylon brush and long, smooth strokes, apply the glue mixture evenly over the surface of the panel. When finished, rinse the brush immediately in tepid water to clean.

Let the glue coat dry thoroughly. (This may take as long as 3 to 4 days, depending on the humidity.)

4. When the glue coat is dry, apply a coat of pink latex to the panel surface using long, even strokes. Draw each stroke down the entire length of the panel; do not brush over an already painted area. This coat of paint will begin to crackle after 20 to 30 seconds.

Allow the paint to dry for 24 hours or more; then seal the finish with two coats of polyurethane varnish.

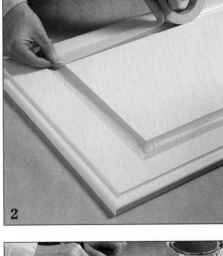

START TO FINISH

Comb painting is among the most versatile of all painted finishes, and combed patterns are some of the fastest to apply. Ranging from the random strokes of a fantasy wood grain to more purposeful patterns—like the faux malachite design, *opposite*—combing is simple to do and nearly foolproof.

The design is created by painting a contrasting color over a dry base coat, then raking through the wet top layer of paint with various sizes of combs to allow the base color to show through.

Combs can be metal graining tools from a paint shop or art supply store. Or, make your own combs from cardboard or plastic squeegees. The teeth should be regularly spaced and should vary in width from comb to comb, from ⅛ to ¾ of an inch.

It's the width of the comb's teeth and the direction of the raking motion that determine the overall design. That design might be curves, stripes, swirls, or just plain squiggles.

To re-create the faux malachite finish on these nesting tables (so-called because the color and pattern was inspired by that most precious of semiprecious stones), use white and seafoam green for the base coat and a deeper green for the second coat.

1. After sanding and priming the piece, apply a base coat of seafoam green and white high-gloss, oil-base paint. It is very important to mottle the colors, creating light and dark gradations across the surface, so that you get color variations in the pattern once the combing is completed.

2. Assemble a variety of combs with different size teeth, such as those shown *below*.

Once the base coat is dry, apply a thin glaze of dark green acrylic paint. The paint can be thinned with water to the consistency of light cream, if necessary. Because the acrylic paint will dry very quickly, apply the paint to only a small section at a time, then comb immediately.

3. During the combing process, work alternately with the various sizes of combs. Put enough pressure on the combs to cut through the dark green and allow the base coat of seafoam and white to show through.

Work from one corner of the piece to the other, building a pattern of swirls, one upon another. Keep in mind that real malachite forms concentric circles around circles and ovals, like the overlapping ripples of a series of small stones dropped close together in a pool.

4. Comb all surfaces of the piece—edges, sides, legs, rungs—striving to keep a sense of rhythmic but nonsymmetrical patterning throughout.

Once the project is completed, seal the finish with several coats of polyurethane, sanding lightly between coats.

START TO FINISH

Vinegar painting is an appealing technique, one akin to the free and easy finger painting we all loved to do in kindergarten. It was developed by nineteenth-century country crafters striving to meet their clients' demands for fancy finishes on furniture and woodwork.

This technique is quick and nearly foolproof, particularly suitable for decorating large, flat surfaces. What's more, the materials are inexpensive and readily available.

Traditionally, vinegar-painted designs were broad and fanciful—no real effort was made to imitate actual wood grains or other natural patterns.

The vinegar-paint solution readily takes impressions from almost any material: wadded plastic wrap, paper towels, corks, sponges, plastic modeling clay, a crumpled rag, or the tip of a finger. The more imaginative the tool, the more intriguing the pattern.

You usually have about 15 minutes in which to experiment with designs before the paint dries. If you don't like the results, just wipe the surface clean with a rag dipped in clear vinegar and start all over again. The final finish must be protected with several coats of varnish.

1. To begin, assemble the following materials: sandpaper and sanding sealer; primer and semigloss white enamel paint; white vinegar and white sugar; powdered poster or tempera paints in your choice of colors; liquid dishwashing detergent; paintbrushes; plastic wrap for patterning; measuring cup and spoons; and spray varnish.

Sand the piece lightly and apply a coat of sanding sealer. Coat the piece with primer and give it a base coat of white semigloss enamel; let dry.

2. Next, make a solution of ¼ cup white vinegar, ½ teaspoon sugar, and a few drops of liquid detergent. In a separate container, mix 2 tablespoons of powdered tempera or poster paint in a color of your choice (we used French blue) with enough of the vinegar solution to form a paste. Continue adding vinegar solution and stirring until the paint is the consistency of cream.

Apply the vinegar solution to one section of the piece at a time.

3. While the paint is still wet, dab the paint with a wadded piece of plastic wrap. To remove drips, dab a soft cloth in clear vinegar and wipe away the dribbles.

4. For the dot designs on the cabinet door, first paint the surface with blue vinegar paint. Then use the tip of your finger to create circular dots at regular intervals. Press your finger on the painted surface, swivel slightly, and lift it straight up. (Wipe finger on a paper towel between dabs.) If the paint dries before you finish, repaint the surface and complete the dot design.

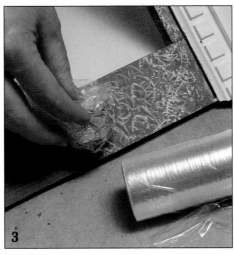

START TO FINISH

Tortoiseshell was first used as an ornamental veneer in the Orient. As the vogue for all things oriental swept through Europe in the seventeenth and eighteenth centuries, many Venetian, French, English, and even colonial American craftspersons worked to create painted finishes that would mimic the mottled shadings and distinctive colorings of this precious material.

Successful versions of tortoiseshell finishes range from careful renderings in a natural-istic style to fantasy patterns—like the tongue-in-cheek treatment, *opposite*—to those that merely suggest the shadings, luminosity, and movement of the orig-inal material.

Traditionally, a tor-toiseshell finish is used in small areas and painted only on flat or gently rounded surfaces and on surfaces to which real tortoiseshell veneer might actually have been applied. But modern-day enthusiasts delight in applying this whimsical finish to a much greater variety of surfaces, from dining room chairs to baseboards.

The ground for a tor-toiseshell finish like that on this ladder-back chair should be gold or a light, sharp yellow. The mottling is done with three shades of gold and amber oil paint (burnt umber, burnt sienna, and raw sienna), and accented with black.

Begin by lightly sanding the piece of furniture, then apply one or two coats of primer.

1. Using high-gloss house paint, brush on a base coat of gold. The precise shade of the base coat (light, medium, or dark) determines the lightness of the tortoiseshell finish. Allow the base coat to dry thoroughly.

2. Prepare a varnish and oil mixture of one part linseed oil to one part clear varnish. Using a small, round brush, first dip the brush into the varnish/oil mixture, then dab it into one of the gold or amber oil paints. Press the brush against the wood surface and drag it downward, making a short, diagonal stroke. Paint the entire surface of the piece with these short, diagonal strokes, alternating among the three shades of gold/amber oil paint (raw sienna, burnt umber, burnt sienna). Add accent strokes of black, dipping the brush in the same oil/varnish mixture before each black stroke.

3. As you dab on this second layer of color, be sure to use enough oil/varnish mixture with each stroke to give it a transparent quality. The base coat color always should be visible beneath each stroke of gold, amber, or black.

4. When the painted piece is completely dry, apply a thin, light glaze of polyurethane sealer that is tinted with several drops of burnt umber oil paint. If the glaze appears to be too light in color, apply a second coat after the first coat is dry. Lightly sand between coats.

COTTAGE CHARM

◆

A SWEET APPEALING KIND OF GRACE

In colonial times, exotic materials were beyond the reach of most, so accommodating crafters devised clever ways to give humbler stuff the look of fine-grained woods and carved detailing. Try their tricks to turn nondescript furnishings into heirlooms.

COTTAGE CHARM

Still-life paintings of fruit and flowers like these were extremely popular in nineteenth-century America. Most were created with the aid of stencils—called theorems—and were painted by earnest young ladies practicing the "gentle arts" in female seminaries, or by girls and housewives who delighted in painting these "fancy pieces" as gifts for friends or to decorate their own homes.

Though many theorem paintings were on watercolor paper or parchment, painting on velvet also was extremely popular.

The "Tulips in Salt-Glazed Pot" and "Apple, Pear, and Plum" designs, *left,* are contemporary versions of traditional theorem subjects, painted with artist's oils on cotton velveteen fabric.

Fanciful wood-grain patterns like those on the picture frames were among the most popular of all faux finishes in the late eighteenth and early nineteenth centuries. Although some artists strove to reproduce an exact replica of a given wood grain—bird's-eye maple or burled chestnut, for example—most simply aimed for a generic wood-grain effect. The elegant table on page 53 and the folk art wood frames, *left,* are both examples of the latter approach.

To achieve this effect, the piece is first painted with a light-colored base coat, usually yellow ocher, and allowed to dry. Next, a contrasting color is brushed over the entire surface and, while the paint is still wet, the artist drags a feather or other tool across the painted surface to create a pattern.

Different tools yield different effects, of course; the tool used on both the chest and the sides of the picture frames was a goose quill. To create the fanlike pattern on the corner blocks of each frame, the artist dragged a forefinger across the wet paint in lines radiating out from the inside corner of the block, then finished the design with a thumbprint placed at the point from which the spokes fan out on each block.

The instructions for these paintings begin on page 60.

COTTAGE CHARM

The primitive portrait of "George General Washington and Lady Washington" that inspired the adaptations at *left* is among the best-known and best-loved examples of the fraktur-style painting practiced by the German-speaking folk who settled in southeastern Pennsylvania. The original portrait, painted about 1775–1800, is now part of the Abby Aldrich Rockefeller folk art collection in Williamsburg, Virginia.

Our contemporary copy, *top left,* painted in acrylics on parchment-like paper and tucked into a folk-art-inspired frame, makes a charming accent piece for any country-style room.

Another version of the same couple trims the wall-hung game board *below.*

Opposite is a superb example of the wood-grainer's art. Here, the graining is used only on the top and drawer front of the table, creating a striking contrast with the frame that is painted a deep green. We used a new, unfinished wood table for this project, but the same procedure can be applied to any secondhand piece. See pages 63–66 for how-to instructions.

COTTAGE CHARM

Familiar folk motifs are given a refreshing new twist on the chest, *opposite*. Sketched with broad wit and a bold brush, this parade of hearts and tulips, rabbits, and stars transforms an ordinary chest into a piece of modern-day folk art. The antiqued palette of blue-gray, gold, and deep red is comfortably traditional, but this exuberant piece would add a touch of class to any decor.

Beneath the chest lies a painted floorcloth of diagonal design—squares of creamy white alternate with blocks of richly veined and marbled tartan green. As shown, the finished cloth measures approximately 2x3½ feet, but the pattern can easily be adapted to suit any size floorcloth.

The "Black Knight" floorcloth *above* also features alternating blocks of color arranged on the diagonal. A sassy striped red border frames and defines the bold black and white design. Easy to lay out and paint, this pattern can be worked up in any combination of colors. Instructions for these projects begin on page 66.

COTTAGE CHARM

A deep blue, sponge-painted finish emblazoned with stenciled motifs and a medallion monogram turns a utilitarian silver chest into this handsome piece *below*. The techniques are simple, the results spectacular.

Sponge painting is but one of many fantasy finishes popular with artists and crafters in nineteenth-century America. Like wood-grain designs, sponging requires the application of an initial, light-colored base coat (in this case, royal blue latex enamel) that is brushed on and allowed to dry. A second, darker color (here, navy blue) is then patted on with gentle dabs of a blotted sponge.

When the sponge-painted background is dry, the tulip and leaf designs and the monogram are stenciled on in cream-colored enamel. Light sanding and a brushed-on, wiped-off coat of dark oak stain give the finished piece a pleasingly antique patina.

Beautifully wrought needlework screens were treasured accessories in aristocratic homes of colonial America. The floral painted fire screen, *opposite,* is a re-creation of the gay patterning and mottled textures of a fine petit point design in a folk art fashion.

First paint the blossoms in brilliant acrylics against an off-white, latex enamel base coat. To create the antiqued mottling around the edges of the screen, sponge-paint its perimeter with burnt umber, shading in to cream toward the center of the design. See pages 70 and 72 for the how-to instructions for these two projects.

Cottage Charm

Here are two handsome birds of quite a different feather which are perfect folk art accents for your yard or porch.

Whirligigs, or wind toys like the Canada goose *at left,* were popular amusements for both children and adults from the mid-1800s onward.

This classic whirligig features a pair of rotating wings with beautiful comb-painted "feathers." Set on his own stand with his outstretched wings in perpetual flight, he stands 30 inches tall.

Whimsies—free-standing figures carved from a single piece of wood—were nineteenth-century oddments meant to entertain or amuse, or to exhibit a craftsperson's special skills. And the 24-inch-tall whimsical barnyard rooster, *below,* does both.

All poised to crow, he looks best cut from a single weathered barn board. Stamp him all over with potato-print "feathers" in several different shades of paint. See pages 75 and 76 for instructions to make these fine birds.

Faux-Finished Chest

Shown on page 49.

MATERIALS

Purchased small wood chest with flat top and sides (ours measures 7½x8x10¾ inches)
Medium- and fine-grit sandpapers
Tack cloth
Black latex enamel
White primer paint
Gesso
Spackling compound
Yellow ocher acrylic paint
Alizarine crimson tube watercolor
1½-inch-wide flat Chinese bristle brush
Goose quill
Satin varnish
Paintbrush for varnish

INSTRUCTIONS

Note: Before you begin this project, read all instructions carefully. Practice the faux-finish steps on scrap wood to familiarize yourself with the technique and the use of the goose quill.

PREPARATION: Sand the chest using the medium-grit sandpaper. Fill in holes and dents with spackling compound. Sand again using the fine-grit sandpaper. Wipe all surfaces with a tack cloth.

Apply a coat of white primer paint to the inside of the chest and let dry. Paint primed surfaces black.

Coat the outside surfaces with gesso. When gesso is dry, sand lightly with fine sandpaper until smooth. Paint the chest with two coats of yellow ocher. Allow paint to dry thoroughly between coats.

GRAINING: Squeeze a small dab of alizarine crimson onto the center of the lid. Sprinkle a few drops of water onto the pigment to thin it so it can be easily spread. Do not allow the paint to become watery. Brush the paint mixture evenly over the lid's top surface.

Beginning at the center, drag the edge of the quill feathers through the paint mixture in wavy concentric circles. The quill may be twisted, turned, or zigzagged through the

paint to achieve different effects. The resulting grain lines should resemble those on a crosscut log.

After the basic grain lines are completed, accent three or four of the grain circles at random using the Chinese bristle brush. Dab the dry brush along the circle for a blurred effect. Dab the center of the lid where the concentric circles begin.

Paint the remaining four sides, one at a time, preparing each like the lid. Begin the graining steps in the middle of the lower edge on these surfaces. Drag the quill in elongated half circles, referring to the photo on page 49. Use the Chinese bristle brush to dab random half circles as desired.

Thin alizarine crimson with water to paint the lid and opening edges and the base. Apply the thinned paint using light strokes to simulate a straight grain.

FINISHING: When grained surfaces are dry, apply two thin coats of varnish, allowing varnish to dry thoroughly between coats.

Theorem Paintings

Shown on page 50.
Framed tulip picture is 11⅜x12⅜ inches. Framed fruit picture is 10⅜x11¾ inches.

MATERIALS
For the paintings
Stencil acetate
Crafts knife
Tracing paper
Fine-point black marker
No. 2 stencil brush
Remnant of off-white velveteen
9x15-inch piece of foam-core board
Artist's oil paints in the following colors: Red, dark blue, royal blue, dark green, black, and yellow
Paper palette
Palette knife
Paint thinner
Black india ink
Crow quill pen
Masking tape
Scissors
White glue

For the frames
7¼x8⅛-inch piece of glass for tulip picture
6¼x7-inch piece of glass for fruit picture
Two *each* of ⅜-inch clear pine pieces in the following dimensions: 2½x12⅜-inch, 2½x11⅜-inch, 2x12⅜-inch, and 2x11⅜-inch for the tulip picture
Two *each* of ⅜-inch clear pine pieces in the following dimensions: 2½x11¾-inch, 2½x10⅜-inch, 2x11¾-inch, and 2x10⅜-inch for the fruit picture
Eight 2½-inch-square pieces of ¼-inch clear pine for the corner blocks
Miter box
Wood glue
Finishing nails
Medium- and fine-grit sandpaper
Tack cloth
Gesso
Spackling compound
Yellow ocher acrylic paint
Burnt umber tube watercolor
1½-inch flat Chinese bristle brush
Goose quill
Satin varnish
Paintbrush for varnish
Eight push points

INSTRUCTIONS
GENERAL DIRECTIONS: In theorem painting the patterns are referred to as "master drawings." Each area of the drawing is numbered so that no two adjacent areas have the same number. Stencils are cut from this numbered drawing with one stencil made for each set of numbered areas.

For all stenciling projects, first trace the whole pattern onto tracing paper with a fine-point marker. Secure the tracing with tape to a flat work surface. Then position and tape a piece of acetate over the tracing and trace the outline of the numbered area to be cut away.

When a design requires more than one cut stencil, always trace the cutting line for one stencil pattern on the acetate with *solid lines* and the surrounding design with *dashed lines* (registration marks).
continued

FULL·SIZE
PATTERN

THEOREM PAINTINGS

61

The dashed lines serve as guides and ensure accuracy when you position successive stencil patterns atop previously stenciled areas.

Label each acetate stencil (first, second, third, and so on) to designate the sequence of stenciling steps as noted in the directions.

Lay the acetate atop a cutting board and cut out the design with the crafts knife. Always allow at least a 1-inch border around the cut edge of each stencil.

When stenciling theorem paintings, concentrate the pigment near the edges of the stencil. This gives the painted area dimension.

For the tulip painting

Cut a 7¼x8⅛-inch rectangle from foam-core board and a 9¼x10⅛-inch rectangle from velveteen. Cover the foam-core board with the velveteen, gluing the excess fabric to the back of the core.

Referring to the pattern at the *top* of page 61, trace the separate elements and the registration marks and cut the patterns as follows:

Stencil 1: Cut the areas marked 1 on the master drawing.

Stencil 2: Cut the areas marked 2 on the master drawing.

Stencil 3: Cut the areas marked 3 on the master drawing.

Stencil 4: Cut the areas marked 4 on the master drawing.

STENCILING THE PICTURE: Place the fabric-covered board faceup on the work surface. Center the master drawing tracing atop the board. Lay Stencil 1 atop the tracing in line with the master drawing design. Tape the stencil in place; slide the master drawing out from under the stencil.

Squeeze a small amount of red onto the palette and paint the tulips. Using a nearly dry brush, work the pigment from the edges toward the center of each area.

Thin black paint with thinner and paint the salt-glazed crock. Leave the crock's center very pale gray.

Continuing to use the master pattern as a guide, complete the remainder of the painting with the cut stencils as follows:

Stencil 2, paint the inner tulips red (concentrating the pigment at the upper edge), stems green, and crock design royal blue.

Stencil 3, paint leaves green.

Stencil 4, paint crock rim gray.

If desired, paint the lower portion of the painting green, as shown in the photograph on page 50, to represent a tabletop.

Add the painting details using india ink and the crow quill pen. Outline the crock, crock rim, and stems. Draw an additional pair of lines ⅛ inch down from the crock rim. Make two short stamens on each tulip and vein lines in the center of each leaf.

For the fruit painting

Cut a 6⅛x7-inch rectangle from foam-core board and an 8⅛x9-inch rectangle from velveteen. Cover the foam-core board with velveteen and glue the excess fabric to the back of the core.

Referring to the pattern at *bottom* on page 61, trace the elements and registration marks and cut the stencil patterns as follows:

Stencil 1: Cut the areas marked 1 on the master drawing.

Stencil 2: Cut the areas marked 2 on the master drawing.

STENCILING THE PICTURE: Place the fabric-covered board faceup on the work surface and position Stencil 1 as directed for the stenciling of the tulip picure, *left*.

Using a nearly dry brush, paint the pear yellow, leaf green, and left half of plum dark blue.

Paint the remainder of the design with Stencil 2 as follows: Paint the apple red. Paint the right side of the plum dark blue, concentrating the blue pigment along the curved outside edge.

Mix yellow with green and dab the mixture very lightly around the base of the fruit.

Add details using india ink and the crow quill pen. Make pear and apple stems, leaf stem and veins, and a curly vine. (Refer to the photograph on page 50 for approximate vine placement.)

For the frames

For each frame, miter the ends of *each* 2½-inch-wide pine piece. Glue and nail the ends to create a rectangular frame. Countersink the nails and allow the glue to dry. Repeat using the 2-inch-wide pieces.

Glue the narrower frame rectangle atop the wider frame rectangle, aligning outer edges. The 2½-inch-wide side is the front of the finished frame and the 2-inch-wide side is the back. Do not attach the corner blocks until the painting of the frame is completed.

FAUX PAINTING THE FRAMES: *Note:* Before beginning this part of the project, read all instructions carefully. Practice the faux-finish technique on scrap wood to familiarize yourself with the technique and handling of the goose quill. These directions apply to both frames.

Sand the frame and corner blocks smooth using first medium- and then fine-grit sandpaper. Fill in any holes or dents with spackling compound. Sand until smooth and wipe with a tack cloth. Coat the pieces with gesso; let dry. Sand lightly again.

Paint the frame and blocks with two coats of yellow ocher on top and side edges, allowing paint to dry thoroughly between coats.

Working with the frame only, squeeze a small amount of burnt umber onto the center of each side of the frame. Sprinkle a few drops of water onto the pigment to thin it so it can be easily spread. Do not allow the paint to become watery. Brush the paint mixture over the frame's entire top surface.

Beginning at one corner, drag the edge of the quill feathers through the paint mixture in wavy lines, moving diagonally down one side. The quill may be twisted, turned, or zigzagged across the paint to achieve a fanciful wood-grain finish. Repeat this step on all sides of the frame.

Apply pigment and water to one corner block as for the frame. Brush mixture over the top surface. Using your forefinger, drag the pigment across the block in lines fanning out from one corner. Each line will overlap the previous one. Refer to the photograph on page 50 for the desired effect. When the lines are completed, make a thumbprint at the corner where the lines begin. Repeat these instructions on the remaining three blocks.

For the edges of the frame and corner blocks, thin burnt umber with water. Paint each edge using the Chinese bristle brush and regular strokes to simulate a straight wood grain.

When pieces are dry to touch, glue a corner block atop each frame corner, aligning edges.

Apply two thin coats of varnish, allowing varnish to dry thoroughly between coats.

FINISHING: Place the glass and then the painting in the frame from the back. Secure the painting with a push point on each side and cover the back with brown paper.

Faux-Finished Table
Shown on page 53.

MATERIALS
Purchased wood table with
   smooth, flat top and front
   drawer (ours measures
   19½x24x30½ inches)
Medium- and fine-grit sandpapers
Tack cloth
White primer paint
Dark green flat latex enamel
Gesso
Spackling compound
Yellow ocher acrylic paint
Alizarine crimson tube watercolor
1½-inch-wide flat Chinese bristle
   brush
Goose quill
Satin varnish
Paintbrush for varnish
3-inch length of ⅛-inch-diameter
   dowel
Draftsman's compass

INSTRUCTIONS
Note: Before beginning this project, read all instructions carefully. You may wish to practice the faux-finish technique on scrap wood to familiarize yourself with the technique and handling of the goose quill.

PREPARATION: Sand the entire table using medium-grit sandpaper. Fill any holes and dents with spackling compound, sand smooth with fine-grit sandpaper, and wipe with tack cloth. Coat the table base *except* the drawer front with the white primer paint and let dry. Next, coat the tabletop and drawer front with gesso; let dry. Sand lightly again.

Apply two coats of dark green paint to the table base, allowing paint to dry thoroughly between coats. Paint the top of the table and the drawer front with two coats of yellow ocher.

GRAINING: Squeeze a small dab of alizarine crimson onto the center of the tabletop. Sprinkle a few drops of water onto the pigment to thin it so it can be easily spread. Do not allow the paint to become watery. Brush the mixture evenly over the surface of the tabletop.

Beginning at the center, drag the edge of the quill feathers through the paint mixture in wavy concentric circles. The quill may be twisted, turned, or zigzagged through the paint to achieve different effects. The resulting grain lines should simulate those seen on a crosscut log. Refer to the photograph on page 53 for ideas.

After the basic grain lines are completed, accent three or four of the grain circles at random using the Chinese bristle brush. Dab the dry brush along the circle for a blurred effect. Dab the center of the table (where the concentric circles begin) in the same manner.

For the decorative stripe around the perimeter of the tabletop, the wet paint mixture is dragged away, allowing the base color to show through. Insert the dowel piece into the draftsman's compass. Align the compass point shaft with the table edge and spread the compass so the dowel end hits the tabletop 1 inch in from the edge. Keeping the point shaft snug against the table edge and dragging the dowel tip along the top, make a stripe along each side. Begin and end each stripe 1 inch from the perpendicular side so all stripe ends meet.

Repeat the graining procedure for the drawer front, using the drawer pull placement as the center. Add a decorative stripe to the drawer using the same technique as for the tabletop.

For the edges of the tabletop and drawer and for the drawer pull, thin alizarine crimson with water. Paint, using light strokes to simulate a straight wood grain. The front of the knob should be brushed using a circular motion.

FINISHING: When grained surfaces are dry, apply two thin coats of varnish, allowing varnish to dry thoroughly between coats.

Lady and General Washington Game Board
Shown on page 52.
Game board is 15½x24 inches.

MATERIALS
1x15½x24-inch clear pine board
Band saw; router
Sandpaper
Foam egg carton (for thinning
   paints)
Nos. 1, 2, and 6 flat and No. 2
   round artist's brushes; liner
   brushes
Paintbrush for background color,
   stain, and varnish
Acrylic paints in the following
   colors: White, ivory, flesh, tan,
   dark brown, black, green, dark
   gray-blue, slate blue, royal blue,
   red-orange, and dark red
Dark walnut stain
Satin varnish

INSTRUCTIONS
PREPARATION: Trace the full-size top game board pattern on page 64 onto a folded piece of heavy paper; cut out.

continued

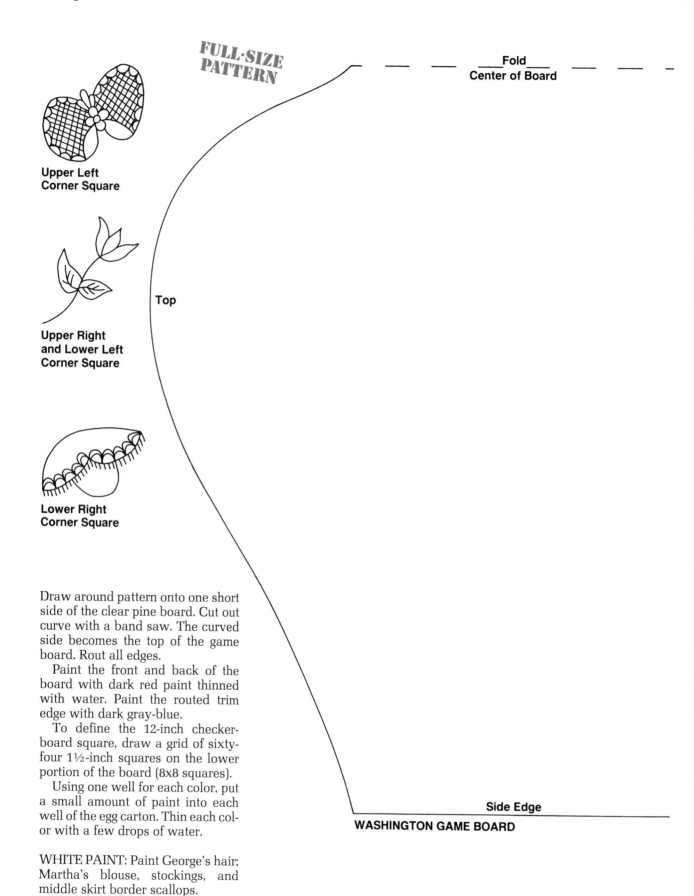

FULL-SIZE PATTERN

**Upper Left
Corner Square**

**Upper Right
and Lower Left
Corner Square**

Top

**Lower Right
Corner Square**

**Fold
Center of Board**

Side Edge

WASHINGTON GAME BOARD

Draw around pattern onto one short side of the clear pine board. Cut out curve with a band saw. The curved side becomes the top of the game board. Rout all edges.

Paint the front and back of the board with dark red paint thinned with water. Paint the routed trim edge with dark gray-blue.

To define the 12-inch checkerboard square, draw a grid of sixty-four 1½-inch squares on the lower portion of the board (8x8 squares).

Using one well for each color, put a small amount of paint into each well of the egg carton. Thin each color with a few drops of water.

WHITE PAINT: Paint George's hair; Martha's blouse, stockings, and middle skirt border scallops.

WASHINGTON PICTURE

IVORY PAINT: Paint the scalloped skirt band middle stripe on Martha's dress; George's breeches and closures on coat.

FLESH PAINT: Paint hands and faces of both figures.

TAN PAINT: Paint Martha's dress and hat tan *except* the scalloped skirt band, skirt border scallops, and hat trim. In additon, paint George's shirt and the two large flower center petals.

GREEN PAINT: Paint Martha's hat plume and all flower leaves.

RED-ORANGE PAINT: Paint rosy cheeks on both figures; Martha's hat flower, flower in hand, and top skirt border scallops; George's coat trim and remaining flower petals.

SLATE BLUE PAINT: Paint the small scallops on Martha's skirt band and George's stockings.

ROYAL BLUE PAINT: Paint Martha's remaining hat, skirt, and blouse trim, and George's coat.

BLACK PAINT: Paint both figures' shoes, all the flower stems, and George's hat.

continued

65

DARK RED AND WHITE PAINTS: Add dark red and white scallops to George's hat brim.

DARK BROWN PAINT: Carefully paint all detail using the liner brush. If desired, the writing may be done in black or dark brown.

CHECKER GRID: Outline the grid with dark brown, and paint alternate squares dark gray-blue. Trace and transfer the corner motif patterns on page 64 to the appropriate corner squares. Paint the motifs following the instructions on page 65 for the similar motifs on the figures.

FINISHING: Brush the dark walnut stain over the top and edges of the game board. Let the stain set for one minute; wipe off excess using a clean cloth.

Apply two coats of varnish to game board, allowing varnish to dry thoroughly between coats.

General and Lady Washington Picture

Shown on page 52.
Finished picture, unframed, is 8x8¼ inches.

MATERIALS

8x8¼-inch piece of parchment
Foam egg carton (for thinning paints)
Carbon paper
No. 2 round and Nos. 1 and 2 flat artist's brushes; liner brushes
Acrylic paints in the following colors: White, ivory, flesh, tan, dark brown, black, green, royal blue, slate blue, and red-orange

INSTRUCTIONS

PREPARATION: Transfer the full-size pattern and wavy border on page 65 to the parchment using carbon paper.

Using one well for each color, put a small amount of paint into each well of the egg carton. Add water to thin each color to the consistency of ink. Test the colors for adequate coverage on a scrap of paper before beginning. If necessary, add more

paint. Refer to the photo on page 52 for color placement as you proceed with the painting instructions that follow.

WHITE PAINT: Paint George's hair and outer hat trim scallops; Martha's underblouse, stockings, and hat flower center.

IVORY PAINT: Paint George's breeches; Martha's middle skirt border between the scalloped edges and the middle band of the scalloped border along the skirt hem.

FLESH PAINT: Paint hands and faces of both figures.

TAN PAINT: Paint Martha's dress and hat tan *except* for the scalloped skirt band, the skirt border scallops, and hat trim. In addition, paint George's shirt, coat closures, and the two large flower center petals.

GREEN PAINT: Paint Martha's left and right hat plume segments and all flower leaves.

RED-ORANGE PAINT: Paint rosy cheeks on both figures and Martha's hat plume center, flower in hand, and skirt border top scallops; George's hat scallops, coat trim, and remaining flower petals.

SLATE BLUE PAINT: Paint the small scallops on Martha's scalloped skirt border and George's stockings.

ROYAL BLUE PAINT: Paint Martha's remaining hat, skirt, and blouse trim, and George's coat.

BLACK PAINT: Paint both figures' shoes, George's hat, and all the flower stems.

DARK BROWN PAINT: Carefully line and paint all details using the liner brush.

FINISHING: To give the finished painting a matted look, paint the area outside the border with a slightly thicker mixture of dark blue.
Frame as desired.

Painted Rabbit Chest

Shown on cover and on page 54.

MATERIALS

Purchased wooden chest measuring at least 10x26 inches on the front surface, for rabbit and heart design (ours measures 17 inches tall, 28¾ inches wide, and 12¼ inches deep)
White latex primer paint
Latex enamel in the following colors: Dark red, white, black, gold, blue-gray, blue-green, and light green
Black artist's oil paint
Linseed oil
No. 2 round, Nos. 2 and 6 flat, and 1- and 3-inch-wide brushes
Cardboard for templates
Polyurethane satin varnish
Paintbrush for varnish
Graph paper
Sponge

INSTRUCTIONS

Paint the chest inside and out using white primer paint. Apply two coats of blue-green paint to chest, allowing paint to dry thoroughly between coats. Paint trim blue-gray.

Enlarge the rabbit pattern, *bottom opposite,* onto graph paper, transfer to cardboard, and cut out to make a template. Make templates for the full-size heart, star, and tulip motifs, *top opposite.*

Referring to the photo on page 54, trace the pattern shapes onto the chest, centering the rabbit on the front. Center hearts on each corner edge from top to bottom and place a star on each side and on front behind the rabbit.

Referring to photo, trace tulips, adding freehand stems and leaves. Motif placements may be altered to fit your chest.

Paint the rabbit dark red, hearts gold with dark red borders, tulips white, and leaves green. Paint stems black and add black stamens with dark red tips to each tulip. Paint the stars gold. Outline them with dark red, and embellish the side stars with white outside each angle.

continued

Center

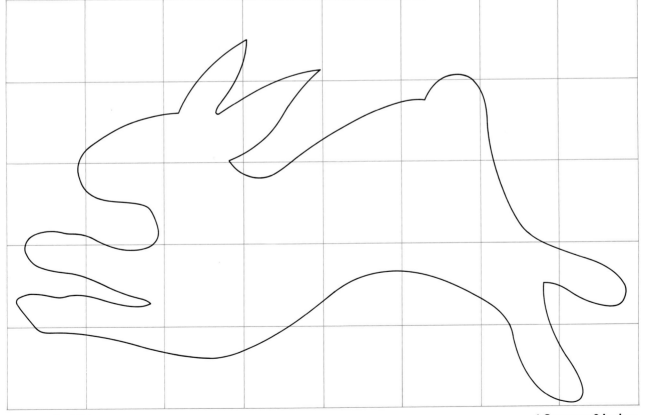

RABBIT CHEST

1 Square = 2 Inches

Add borders of alternating dark red and gold dots along the lid top and chest top and bottom edges.

Thin black oil paint with linseed oil and stain the chest with the resulting color wash. Leave on for one minute; wipe off with a clean cloth.

Dab the rabbit silhouette with a dry sponge dipped in black paint for a stippled effect.

When all paint is dry, apply two coats of varnish to chest, allowing ample drying time between coats.

Black Knight Floorcloth

Shown on page 55.
Finished cloth is 27x41 inches.

MATERIALS
31x45-inch piece of No. 10 cotton canvas
Black and red acrylic paints
Water-base varnish
White latex paint
Yardstick; sharp pencil
¾-inch-wide masking tape
Fabric glue or hot-glue gun
Small packing sponges (dense)
Paintbrush
Fine-grit sandpaper; scissors
Crafts knife
Drop cloth or paper to protect work surface

INSTRUCTIONS
PREPARATION: Prepare cloth following the Preparation instructions for the Diagonal Floorcloth, *right,* except trim the white painted fabric to 29x43 inches.

Hem the cloth following the same instructions. After the hem is glued in place, the cloth should measure 27x41 inches.

Sand the front of the cloth lightly to smooth and remove debris. Brush or vacuum to remove dust from rug.

MARKING THE PAINTING LINES: Measure and draw a line 3 inches in from the hemmed edge all the way around for the outside border. A rectangle measuring 21x35 inches will remain in the center. Referring to the drawing, *top opposite,* mark points 3½ inches from each side of the four corners along the perimeter of the inside rectangle. Then mark 7-inch points consecutively from the corner markings. Use the yardstick to connect the points diagonally across the top of the cloth as shown in the drawing. With a pencil, lightly mark the alternating diamonds with an X to designate the diamonds that will be painted black.

To tape the border, first lay the tape along the outside edges of the marked diamond rectangle to mark off the inner ¾-inch white border. Next, leave a ½-inch area untaped for the red border. Then put masking tape along the outside edge of the red border for the next white ¾-inch border. Leave the remaining area along the edge untaped for the outside black border.

Tape the masking tape along the outside edges of the white squares to protect that space when painting the black diamonds.

Using the crafts knife, trim the overlapping tape from the areas that will be painted. Press down the tape edges with fingertips to prevent paint from spreading into the white painted areas.

PAINTING: Paint the black diamonds in the center rectangle following the Painting instructions for the Diagonal Floorcloth on page 70. Allow paint to dry for one-half hour.

Sponge black paint onto outside border edge of the rug. Clean the sponge thoroughly and squeeze red paint onto the sponge. Apply red to the other untaped border stripe.

FINISHING: Allow the rug to dry overnight. Remove all tape and paint any touch-ups that may be necessary.

Apply three coats of varnish, allowing four hours of drying time between each coat.

Diagonal Floorcloth

Shown on page 54.
Finished cloth is 25½x42½ inches.

MATERIALS
30x47-inch piece of No. 10 cotton canvas
Folk Art paints for marbleizing in the following colors: Tartan green, summer sky, black, and wicker white
Folk Art thickener and extender
Drop cloth or paper to protect work surface
Yardstick; sharp pencil
Scissors; masking tape
Crafts knife
Fabric glue or hot-glue gun
White latex paint; paintbrush
Fine-grit sandpaper
Small packing sponges
Cellulose sponge
Goose feather
Water-base varnish

INSTRUCTIONS
PREPARATION: Thin white latex paint with water until it is the consistency of thick syrup.

Lay a drop cloth over the surface where you are working. Paint the surface (front side) of the canvas fabric. Hang to dry overnight. Apply second and third coats of the white paint, each coat four hours apart.

When paint is thoroughly dry, remeasure and trim the fabric to 27½x44½ inches; precise measurement is important. Turn the piece over. On the back side, measure and mark 2 inches in from the edge all around the cloth. Fold edge of cloth over to meet 2-inch mark, forming a 1-inch hem. Miter corners and finger-press edge to make a sharp crease. Use fabric glue or hot glue to fasten the hem. Turn cloth to right side. The cloth should measure 25½x42½ inches.

Sand the front of the cloth lightly to smooth and remove debris. Brush or vacuum cloth to remove dust.

continued

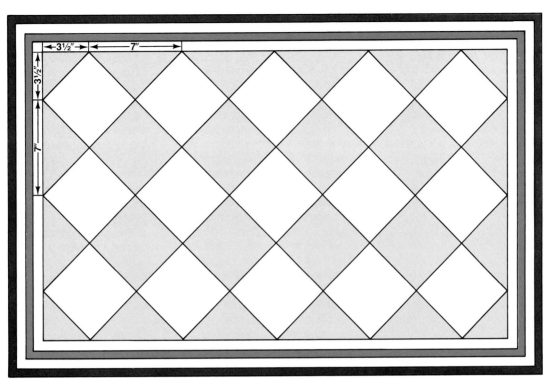

BLACK KNIGHT FLOORCLOTH

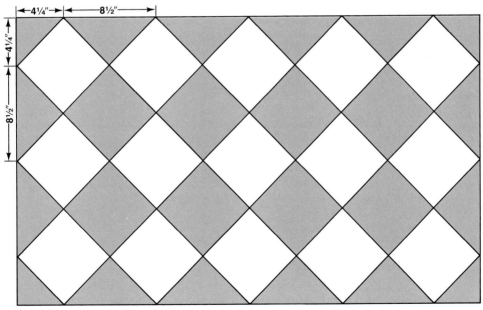

DIAGONAL FLOORCLOTH

MARKING THE DIAMOND GRID: Referring to the drawing on page 69, *bottom,* mark points 4¼ inches from each side of the four corners. Then mark points consecutively 8½ inches from the corner markings. Use the yardstick to connect the points diagonally across the top of the cloth as shown in the drawing. With a pencil, lightly mark the alternating diamonds with an X to indicate the areas that will be painted black.

Tape the masking tape along the outside edges of the white squares to protect that space when painting the black diamonds. With the crafts knife trim the overlapping tape from the areas that will be painted. Press down the tape edges with fingertips to prevent paint from spreading into white areas.

PAINTING: Shake the black acrylic paint to mix. Squeeze some black paint onto a dense sponge, and dab on paper to work paint into sponge. Begin applying paint in the middle of each diamond and continue out toward the taped edges, being careful to brush lightly along these edges; allow paint to dry for one-half hour.

Wet sponge and squeeze water out. Use tweezers to pull off pieces of the sponge from the surface and edges of one side of the sponge; set sponge aside.

MARBLEIZING: Assemble the marbleizing materials as follows: plastic-coated paper plate; goose feather; tartan green, summer sky, and white paints; extender; and thickener.

Shake all paints to mix thoroughly. Squeeze tartan green in a circle onto the plate, approximately 4–6 times around the plate. Add summer sky in the same manner. Squeeze the thickener on top of the colors, going around the plate four times. Add the extender on top of all these mixtures, going around the plate three times.

Pick up the plate and move it around so all the liquids roll together, but do not mix. The paint should not form a solid color.

Place sponge lightly in paint, then lightly on the black squares, first in one direction and then in another, slightly overlapping. Some of the black should show through. The sponging goes very quickly. Refill sponge after every four blottings. *Note:* Check sponge periodically to make sure it doesn't get murky. If it does, wash it out and clean the plate. Begin again with new paint.

VEINING THE RUG: On the same plate of paint (without cleaning it), squeeze a puddle of white paint. Next to the white puddle, squeeze an equal amount of thickener, and on either side of this, make two puddles of extender. Move the plate so the liquids roll around, but do not mix. Dip the point of the feather into the mixture and drag the point and approximately 2 inches of the wider part of the feather through the veining color and marbleizing liquids.

Place the point of the feather on the sponged squares and drag it along the surface to create the vein. For a more natural appearance, make diagonal lines with the feather. Occasionally twist the feather as you drag it to make thicker and thinner parts to the vein.

When all painting is complete, cover the plate with plastic wrap to save and protect it from drying out. Use it for later touch-ups.

FINISHING: Allow the rug to dry overnight. Remove all tape and paint any touch-ups that may be necessary.

Apply three coats of varnish, allowing four hours of drying time between each coat.

Painted Fire Screen
Shown on page 57.

MATERIALS
Purchased new or antique fire screen with a flat front surface measuring at least 19 inches wide and 21 inches tall
White primer paint
Off-white latex enamel
Liquitex acrylic paints in the following colors: Titanium white, unbleached titanium, brilliant yellow, brilliant orange, cerulean blue hue, Hooker's green, phthalocyanine green, burnt umber, Payne's gray, light magenta, naphthol crimson, and brilliant purple
2-inch-wide paintbrush
No. 6 round-tip brush; Nos. 4 and 8 flat artist's brushes; liner brushes
Dark oak water-base stain
Satin acrylic varnish
Small sea sponge
Paper palette for mixing paints
Graph paper
Carbon paper

INSTRUCTIONS
PREPARATION: Paint the fire screen front surface with white primer paint; let dry. Paint the same surface with off-white latex enamel.

Enlarge the pattern, *opposite,* onto graph paper. Transfer pattern to center front of fire screen using carbon paper.

To obtain all colors required for this project, mix paints as follows:

For dark pink, mix light magenta with a small amount of naphthol crimson.

For medium pink, mix dark pink with white.

For yellow-orange, mix brilliant yellow with a small amount of brilliant orange.

For dark blue, mix cerulean blue hue with white; darken with Payne's gray.

continued

FIRE SCREEN

For medium blue, mix cerulean blue hue with white.

For light blue, mix medium blue with white.

For medium purple, mix brilliant purple with white.

For light purple, mix medium purple with white.

For medium brown, mix burnt umber with white.

PAINTING THE DESIGN: Using the round-tip brush and a dabbing motion, base-paint the tall center flower medium blue. (The dabbing motion helps define the flower texture.) Load the brush with dark blue and dab over the medium blue at random, concentrating the dark blue near the tip and base. Repeat dabbing technique with a small amount of light blue through the middle of the flower and at the base next to the dark blue.

Paint the remaining tall flower on the left in the same manner using medium purple, brilliant purple, then light purple.

Base-paint white the large five-petal flower, the folded flower at far right, and the five-petal half flower. Using light magenta, paint the petal accents on the half flower, edge the petals of the folded flower, and paint the entire middle and petal accents of the large five-petal flower. Dab dark pink, then brilliant yellow, then dark pink once more in the middle of the five-petal flower, covering progressively smaller areas each time you change paint colors.

Next, use light magenta to base-paint the smallest five-petal flower and the outside of each bell-shaped flower on the left stalk. Edge and accent the petals of the five-petal flower with medium pink and paint the entire center brilliant yellow. Add a dark pink center atop the yellow. Paint the inside of each bell-shaped flower dark pink. Accent the outside edges using medium pink.

Paint the folded flower on the far left medium pink. Add unbleached titanium shading to the inner petals.

Base-paint the two nine-petal flowers brilliant yellow and add brilliant orange centers. For the top flower, shade the edges of the petals with yellow-orange and stroke tiny yellow-orange lines radiating from the center. For the bottom flower, paint over the yellow petals with yellow-orange, allowing some yellow to show through. Add tiny brilliant orange lines radiating from this flower's center.

Paint the outside of each bell-shaped flower on the right stalk brilliant yellow and the inside of each flower yellow-orange. Accent the outside of each flower as desired to add dimension. Dab brilliant orange along the bottom edge of each flower's inside surface.

Base-paint the remaining five-petal flower medium purple. Paint the entire center and petal accents brilliant purple. Dab medium pink, then dark pink, then brilliant yellow in the middle, covering progressively smaller areas each time.

Paint all the leaves and stems phthalocyanine green. Detail the leaf accents and veins using Hooker's green.

Load the No. 4 brush with burnt umber and paint each basket segment *within* the drawn lines, allowing the off-white paint underneath to create the segment outline detail.

FINISHING: Using the sea sponge, dab burnt umber around the perimeter of the fire screen. With medium brown, overlap the edge of the burnt umber and sponge farther in toward the design using a lighter touch. Repeat the procedure, sponging unbleached titanium up to and around the painted design edges.

When all paint has dried, sand the painted surface very lightly. Allow flecks of off-white paint to show through the motif colors.

Brush on a coat of dark oak stain. Wipe off excess and let dry.

Finish the painted area with a coat of satin varnish.

Stenciled Silver Chest
Shown on page 56.

MATERIALS
Purchased wood silver chest measuring at least 13x19½ inches on the top surface, for stencil and monogram design (ours measures 8½ inches tall, 13¼ inches wide, and 19¾ inches long)

Latex flat enamel paints in the following colors: Royal blue, navy blue, and cream

White primer paint; white chalk

Dark oak stain

Mat varnish

Fine-grit sandpaper

Fine-point marker

Stencil acetate

Crafts knife

½-inch stencil brush

½-inch flat paintbrush

Paintbrush for stain and varnish

Sea sponge

Tracing paper

Graph paper; carbon paper

INSTRUCTIONS
CUTTING THE STENCIL: Begin this project by tracing the full-size stencil border pattern on page 74 onto tracing paper with a fine-point marker. Secure the tracing with tape to a flat work surface. Then position and tape the acetate over the tracing; trace the outline of the area to be cut away. Lay the acetate atop a cutting board and cut out the design with a crafts knife.

PREPARING THE CHEST SURFACE: Sand smooth all surfaces of the chest. Paint the chest inside and out with white primer paint and let dry. Paint the outside surfaces royal blue. When the blue paint is dry, sponge-paint over the royal blue with navy blue paint. To sponge-paint, dip the sponge into a small amount of paint, blot on a paper towel, and dab lightly at random over the prepared surface.

STENCILING THE CHEST: With chalk, mark the center of each edge of the chest lid top surface. The ends

continued

STENCILED CHEST

1 Square = 1 Inch

Cottage Charm

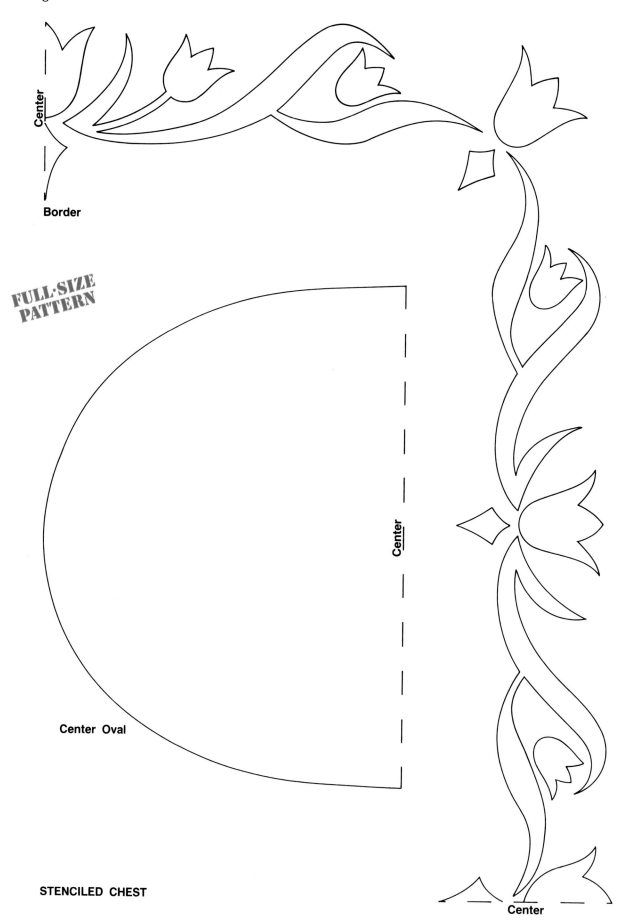

Center

Border

FULL·SIZE
PATTERN

Center

Center Oval

STENCILED CHEST

Center

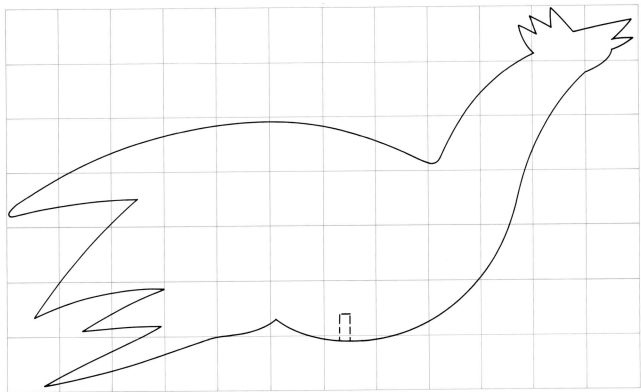

BARNYARD ROOSTER

1 Square = 2 Inches

of the stencil design must be placed in line with these marks so a complete design will be centered on each side of the lid. Place the stencil atop the chest lid in each corner, matching stencil design ends with chalk marks. Lightly draw lines to mark each stencil position, reversing the stencil as necessary for a complete design.

Tape the stencil in place at the upper left corner and paint the design using the stencil brush loaded with cream paint. Move the stencil to the lower left corner position and repeat. Clean the stencil, turn it upside down, and paint the remaining two corners.

For the chest front, center a stencil motif atop each drawer front and paint as for the lid.

PAINTING THE MONOGRAM: Transfer the center oval pattern, *opposite,* to the center of the chest lid with carbon paper.

Enlarge the desired letters from the alphabet on page 73 onto graph paper and make templates. Place the letter shapes atop the oval in the desired monogram arrangement and draw around them. Using the ½-inch flat brush, paint the oval cream leaving the letters blue.

FINISHING: When all paint has dried, sand the entire chest lightly. Allow small flecks of blue to show through the cream paint.

Brush a light coat of dark oak stain over the outer surfaces. Wipe off excess with a soft clean cloth and let dry.

Apply two thin coats of varnish.

Barnyard Rooster

Shown on page 59.
Finished rooster is 14 inches high and 24 inches wide.

MATERIALS
1x14x24-inch piece of barn wood or weathered board
30-inch length of ½-inch-diameter metal rod
4x4x4-inch cedar block for base
Acrylic paints in the following colors: Blue-gray, gray, yellow, and dark red
Paintbrush
Potato
Paring knife
Graph paper
Jigsaw
Weatherproof mat varnish

INSTRUCTIONS
Enlarge the pattern, *above,* onto graph paper and cut out. Draw around the pattern on the wood and cut out the shape with a jigsaw. Drill a ½-inch-diameter hole in the center of the bottom edge for the rod.

Make a wash of blue-gray paint by thinning paint with water. Brush the wash over the sides and edges of the rooster shape.

Cut potato in half crosswise. With a paring knife, carve out the center of each potato half to form a ring design. Dip one cut potato half into gray paint and print rooster body at *continued*

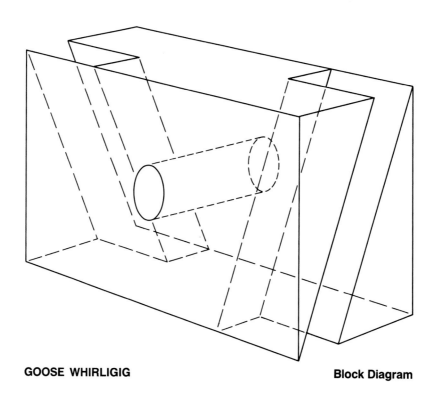

GOOSE WHIRLIGIG   **Block Diagram**

random. Repeat potato printing procedure using the remaining cut potato half and yellow paint.

Paint the beak with a wash of yellow paint and the comb with a wash of dark red.

When paint is dry, brush on a coat of weatherproof varnish.

To mount the rooster, drill a ½-inch-diameter hole 2 inches deep into the center of one side of the cedar block and insert the rod.

Place the rooster atop the remaining rod end and glue in place.

Goose Whirligig
Shown on pages 58 and 59.
Finished size is 26x30 inches,
including base.

MATERIALS
24-inch length of 1x6-inch
  pine (body)
Two 1¼x2-inch pine blocks
  (wings)
Two 1½-inch lengths of ¾-inch
  dowel (spacers)
12x16-inch piece of tempered
  hardboard (wings)
6-inch length of ¼-inch all-thread
  rod
4-inch-long bolt
Two ¼-inch nuts
Two ¼-inch locknuts
Four ¼-inch washers
14-inch length of 1-inch-thick
  dowel
10-inch length of 4x4 lumber (base)
Scroll or band saw
Sandpaper; wood glue
1- and 2-inch flat paintbrushes
Latex flat enamel in the following
  colors: Tan, black, gray, and
  off-white
Weatherproof gloss varnish
Scrap of heavy cardboard (comb
  painting)
Carbon paper; graph paper
Poster board

INSTRUCTIONS
Enlarge the pattern, *opposite,* onto graph paper. Transfer the pattern to the poster board and cut around the outlines to make templates.

Trace the body onto the pine board and four wings onto the hardboard.

WHIRLIGIG PARTS: Cut out the body and wing pieces with a scroll or band saw.

Sand the edges lightly. Drill holes for the wings and axis as indicated on the body pattern.

Make ¼-inch-wide and ½-inch-deep cuts diagonally across the ends of the pine blocks (see block diagram, *above*). Cuts should be made in opposite directions on each of the blocks.

Drill a hole in the center of each block. Position the wings into the diagonal cuts of the blocks and glue in place.

Drill a ¼-inch hole in the centers of the dowel spacers.

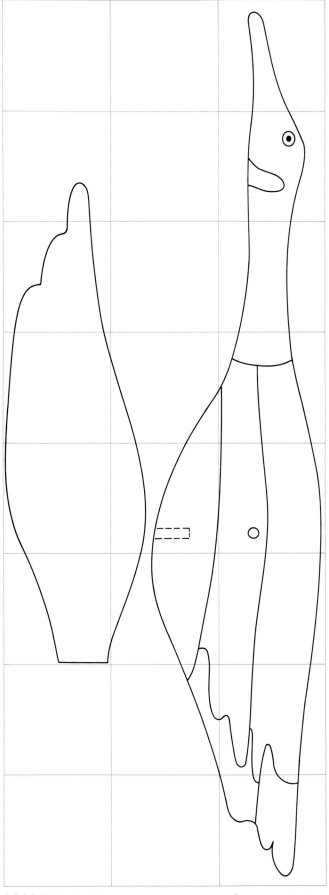

BASE: Drill a 1-inch hole in the center of the base. Insert glue and the 1-inch dowel.

Drill a ¼-inch hole in the center of the upper end of the dowel. Insert the bolt for an axis; cut off the head of the bolt.

PAINTING: Paint the body and wings off-white and the base gray. Referring to the pattern, *left,* sketch the detail lines on the body.

To make a comb for texturing the paint, cut teeth in a 2½x4-inch piece of heavyweight cardboard. Slash-cut the teeth with scissors, making the cuts ½ inch deep and ⅛ inch wide. Space the teeth ¼ inch apart.

Paint the head and upper tail black, stomach gray, and both back sections tan. While the tan paint is still wet, comb through the paint using long wavy strokes to texture the surface.

Treating one side at a time, paint each wing tan and repeat the combing procedure.

When the tan paint on the goose body is dry, paint the upper back section gray and comb through the wet gray paint.

Paint the goose's eye tan with a black center.

Coat all surfaces with weatherproof varnish and let dry.

ASSEMBLY: Insert the all-thread rod through the body. Attach spacers on each side of the body and glue in place.

For each wing, thread a nut, washer, wing, washer, then a locknut onto the all-thread rod.

Do not tighten the locknut, as this will restrict the wing movement.

GOOSE WHIRLIGIG   1 Square = 3 Inches

SIGNS AND SAYINGS

◆

WIT AND WISDOM

Grace your home or gift a friend with one of the charming folk art wall plaques you'll find in this chapter. There are seven designs to choose from, including the heart-shaped tribute to home, above. Some of the signs are witty, some are wise— all are wonderful!

SIGNS AND SAYINGS

A stenciled checkerboard in crisp black and white makes a lively yet easy-to-paint border for the Welcome sign, *left*. Cheerful blossoms in crimson, blue, and yellow sweeten the design.

Feather your nest with the Home Sweet Home sign, *below*. The shaped plaque is easy to cut out with a jigsaw from a 10x14½-inch piece of ¾-inch pine. Use a router to shape the edges as shown, or simply sand them smooth.

Since the trailing vine border on this plaque is produced freehand, you can distribute its graceful swirls and position the robin to complement any shape plaque you may decide to use.

SIGNS AND SAYINGS

More than 150 years ago, John Howard Payne wrote the immortal words,
*'Mid pleasures and
palaces though we
may roam,
Be it ever so humble,
there's no place
like home.*

Home is still a very special place—a place aptly celebrated in this lovely painted plate, with its picket-fenced cottage and simple blessing. It is a handsome piece of folk art that's equally at home hanging on the wall or serving crackers and cheese to a gathering of friends.

Wooden plates of many sizes are available at most crafts shops (this one is 15½ inches in diameter). Once you've prepared the plate with a coat of primer and two coats of background color, it's a simple matter to trace the design elements onto the surface and fill in the details using small and medium-size artist's brushes and colorful acrylic paint.

The instructions for this project begin on page 91.

SIGNS AND SAYINGS

Up until the turn of the century, painted signs bearing shop names or announcing goods and services for sale were as common as billboards across America. Most bore colorful pictures as well as words, since much of the public could not read. And on the domestic scene, hand-stitched samplers proclaiming lofty sentiments or favorite aphorisms hung on the walls of many American homes.

Contemporary versions of those "old tyme" signs and sayings make picturesque accents for any country decor.

Above right is a painted paean to the watermelon—perhaps the quintessential summer fruit. Right beside it is a tongue-in-cheek sampler—painted "stitches" pick out a familiar homily about that all-time favorite American dish, apple pie.

The "Pure Lard" plaque, *opposite,* is stenciled with a motherly sow and five little piglets all nestled in straw. The sign has routed edges for a neat finish and is painted with a drybrush technique to give it a slightly weathered look.

Patterns and instructions for all three signs begin on page 94.

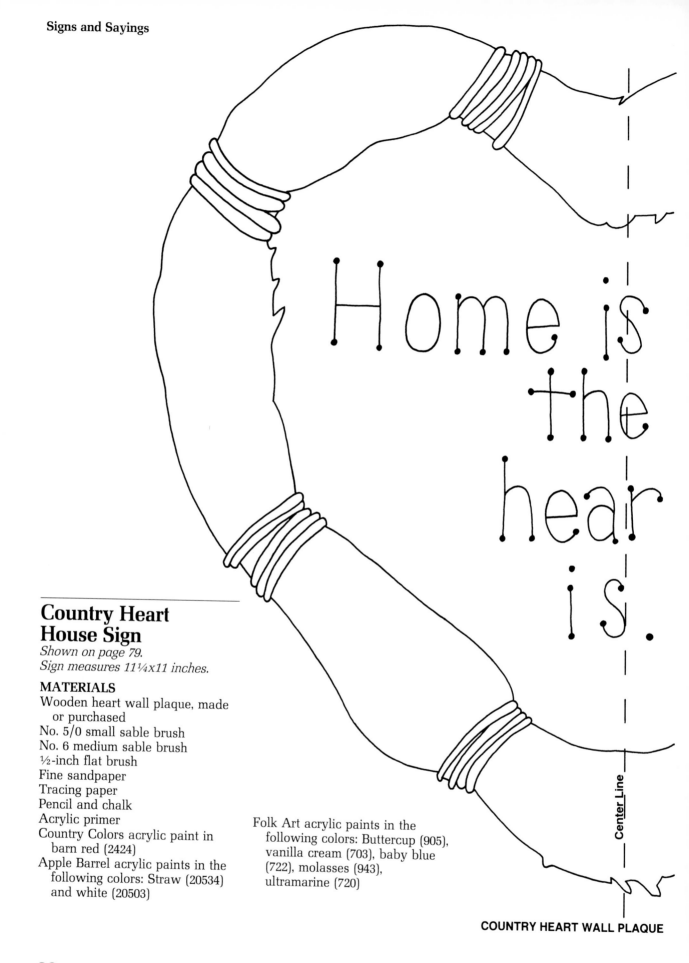

COUNTRY HEART WALL PLAQUE

Center Line

Country Heart House Sign

Shown on page 79.
Sign measures 11¼x11 inches.

MATERIALS
Wooden heart wall plaque, made
  or purchased
No. 5/0 small sable brush
No. 6 medium sable brush
½-inch flat brush
Fine sandpaper
Tracing paper
Pencil and chalk
Acrylic primer
Country Colors acrylic paint in
  barn red (2424)
Apple Barrel acrylic paints in the
  following colors: Straw (20534)
  and white (20503)

Folk Art acrylic paints in the
  following colors: Buttercup (905),
  vanilla cream (703), baby blue
  (722), molasses (943),
  ultramarine (720)

Overlap Center
On Left Half

Center Line

where

INSTRUCTIONS
Note: Allow paint to dry thoroughly before moving to the next step. It is best to use purchased premixed paints for the background to ease necessary touch-ups.

Sand smooth all surfaces of the plaque. Apply one coat of acrylic primer; lightly sand again.

Paint plaque with two coats of barn red.

The full-size pattern for the design is on these two pages. Trace the pattern onto tracing paper. *Note:* To make the complete pattern, align the center dashed lines. The shaded portion, *left,* indicates the overlap area on the two halves. Use this portion to line up the two halves and form the whole pattern.

Color the back of the traced pattern with white chalk. Position pattern, with colored side down, on top of the painted plaque. With a sharp pencil, trace the complete design; remove the pattern.

As you begin to paint the straw heart on the plaque, use a dry brush and do not completely cover the red. Use your brush freely to paint the straw, allowing the colors to define the strands.

continued

Blend a mixture of molasses and straw paints. Use the medium brush to paint strands of straw to define the heart wreath; let paint dry.

Using only the straw color, add more strands of paint to nearly fill the wreath.

Using small amounts of buttercup on a wide *dry* brush, apply wisps of paint over the wreath. Allow the under colors to show through.

Mix small amounts of the vanilla cream and buttercup paints. Use the small brush to stroke in details of the straw pieces. Continue to allow the under colors to show through.

Use the medium brush to dot on baby blue and ultramarine flower centers and to stroke on the white flower petals.

Letter the sign in baby blue paint using the medium brush.

Home Sweet Home Wall Plaque

Shown on page 81.
Finished plaque measures
10x14½ inches.

MATERIALS

10x14½x¾-inch piece of wood, or purchased plaque
Nos. 2 and 00 artist's brushes; ½-inch soft touch-up brush
Acrylic primer
Folk Art acrylic paints in the following colors: Vanilla cream (703), apple-butter brown (820), molasses (943), lemon custard (735), and baby blue (722)
Country Colors acrylic paints in the following colors: Barn red (2424) and stoneware blue (2440)
Apple Barrel acrylic paints in the following colors: Kelly green (20523) and crimson (20533)
Folk Art satin-finish water-base varnish (792)
Folk Art apple-butter brown antiquing water-base acrylic (820)
Fine sandpaper
Tracing paper
Soft lead pencil; soft eraser

INSTRUCTIONS

Note: Allow paint to dry thoroughly before starting the next step. It is best to use purchased premixed paints for the background to ease necessary touch-ups.

Using the full-size pattern, *opposite,* and referring to the photo on page 81, trace the complete saying onto tracing paper. Match position of the bird and the second "home" (top, without nest) on your pattern.

Lightly sand, then paint the plaque with primer. Cover plaque with two coats of vanilla cream.

Color the back of the pattern with the pencil. Place tracing paper, with colored side down, over the painted plaque and draw over all lines to transfer the pattern to the plaque. Remove the tracing paper. Draw the vine freehand, referring to the photo for guidance.

Paint the twig-shaped letters using the No. 2 brush and a mixture of molasses and vanilla cream. Accent the letters with apple-butter brown to give the twigs texture.

Use the No. 00 brush and apple-butter brown to outline and create accents on the letters, and to paint the vine and the bird's legs and feet. Make fine curved strokes randomly through the nest using the same brush and paint.

Paint the eggs baby blue.

Paint leaves on the vine using No. 00 brush and kelly green.

Using barn red and No. 00 brush, stroke over the dark area of the nest containing the painted strokes of apple-butter brown.

For the final color in the nest, use molasses and the No. 00 brush. Brush the paint in curving strokes to give the appearance of a bushy nest.

Use the No. 2 brush and paint the bird's breast lemon custard.

Mix lemon custard, crimson, and a drop of barn red to make orange. Use the orange and the No. 2 brush to create feather marks over the bird's breast area and under beak and eye.

Use No. 2 brush to apply stoneware blue paint over the body (back of head, back, and underbelly).

Speckle the eggs in the nest with stoneware blue.

Paint wing and tail using the No. 2 brush and a mixture of molasses and vanilla cream.

Use the No. 2 brush and dry-brush the bird's body with apple-butter brown.

With No. 00 brush, accent wing and tail with apple-butter brown. Paint eye and beak with same color.

Let dry thoroughly.

Use a soft cloth and apply the apple-butter brown antiquing acrylic to the entire plaque; wipe off excess.

Welcome Sign

Shown on page 80.
Finished sign measures
17x5⅞x¾ inches.

MATERIALS

17x5⅞x¾-inch wooden plaque
Acrylic primer
Folk Art acrylic paints in the following colors: Licorice (938), baby blue (722), ultramarine (720), lemon custard (735)
Apple Barrel acrylic paints in the following colors: White (20503), crimson (20533), kelly green (20523), and straw (20534)
5/0 small sable brush
No. 6 medium sable brush
½-inch-wide flat brush
Stencil brush; crafts knife
Sandpaper; stencil paper
Golden oak stain
Flat spray varnish

INSTRUCTIONS

Sand, then prime plaque with acrylic primer; let dry. Paint with two coats white paint, sanding lightly between coats.

Referring to the full-size patterns on page 90, trace the Stencil Border pattern onto stencil paper. Use the crafts knife to cut out the squares.

Place stencil onto painted plaque, positioning left cut square in upper left-hand corner. With stencil brush, dab lightly with licorice color to paint the squares. Carefully lift stencil; reposition it to paint the next set

HOME SWEET HOME PLAQUE

of squares. Continue in this manner across the top. Then complete the second row of squares, offsetting the painted squares one block to the right to form a checkered border. Repeat the stenciling around the remaining three sides of the plaque.

Referring to the drawing of the sign at the top of page 91, and using the full-size patterns on page 90, prepare a complete pattern for the center of the sign by tracing the design elements onto tracing paper.

Color the back of the tracing with a soft lead pencil. Then lay the tracing, colored side down, over the top of the sign and draw over the lines to transfer the pattern to the plaque.

Paint letters with licorice, using the medium brush.

Dry-brush the dandelion with lemon custard, using wide brush.

Use the medium brush to paint the two flowers at the side borders crimson. Accent the center of the

red flowers with five licorice dots. Add two small dashes of licorice at the edge of each of the six petals.

For the two sprigs of little blue flowers near the center bottom of the plaque, use baby blue to paint all but one flower in each sprig. Paint the final flower in each sprig with ultramarine. Dot all flower centers with lemon custard.

Paint all flower stems with kelly green.

continued

89

FULL·SIZE PATTERN

WELCOME PLAQUE

Stencil Border

WELCOME PLAQUE SCHEMATIC

Paint the ¾-inch edges of the plaque with two coats of ultramarine. Add a randomly placed three-dot triangular pattern of crimson around these edges.

FINISHING: Use a soft cloth to wipe on the golden oak stain and use another soft cloth to dab it off unevenly; let dry. Apply one coat of flat spray varnish.

Bless This House Charger Plate

Shown on page 82.
The finished plate measures
15½ inches in diameter.

MATERIALS
15½-inch-diameter wooden plate
No. 5/0 small sable brush
No. 6 medium sable brush
½-inch-wide flat brush
Folk Art acrylic paints in the
    following colors: Ultramarine
    (720), licorice (938), and
    molasses (943)
Apple Barrel acrylic paints in the
    following colors: Liberty blue
    (20563), kelly green (20523), and
    white (20503)
Country Colors acrylic paints in
    the following colors: Apache red
    (2303) and barn red (2424)
Golden oak stain
Flat spray varnish
Tracing paper; light chalk pencil

INSTRUCTIONS
Note: Allow paint to dry thoroughly before starting the next step. It is best to use purchased premixed paints for the background to ease necessary touch-ups.

Lightly sand, then paint the plate white. With wide *dry* brush, speckle liberty blue around edge of plate.

Paint entire front of plate with two coats of ultramarine, leaving a ¼-inch outer edge of speckled blue over white.

Trace the full-size wedge pattern (including the house, sprig, and saying) on page 92 onto tracing paper. Color the back of the pattern with a soft lead pencil. Place tracing, colored side down, over the painted plate and draw over all lines to transfer the pattern to the plate. Then lift the pattern and reposition it to complete the tracing of the triangle border around the outside edges.

Trace the larger heart motif, color it on the back of the tracing, and, referring to the photo on page 82, trace it onto the plate 2 inches in from the plate edge.

Paint the triangles around the outside of the design with two coats of liberty blue.

Use the medium brush to paint all the hearts (around the border and the larger one) with three coats of apache red.

For the vine, use the light chalk pencil to draw a wavy line around plate rim. Use kelly green and the medium brush to paint the vine. Paint almond-shaped leaves alternating along either side of vine. Paint the small sprig below the saying in the same manner as the vine.

Paint the fence and the lower portion of the house with two coats of white. Use the small brush for the fence and the medium brush for the house.

Paint the roof barn red using the medium brush. Accent the roof by painting small vertical dashes of licorice along the bottom edges.

Paint the stones and mortar of the chimney using molasses, licorice, barn red, and white. Blend the colors in various combinations to create a couple different browns and grays. Use the small brush and the brown mixtures to dot the stones in; follow with the gray mixtures to paint in the mortar.

Use the small brush and two coats of white to paint the lettering in the center of the plate.

To mellow the look of the paint, use a soft cloth to wipe on the golden oak stain. Let stain dry and then spray the plaque with flat varnish.

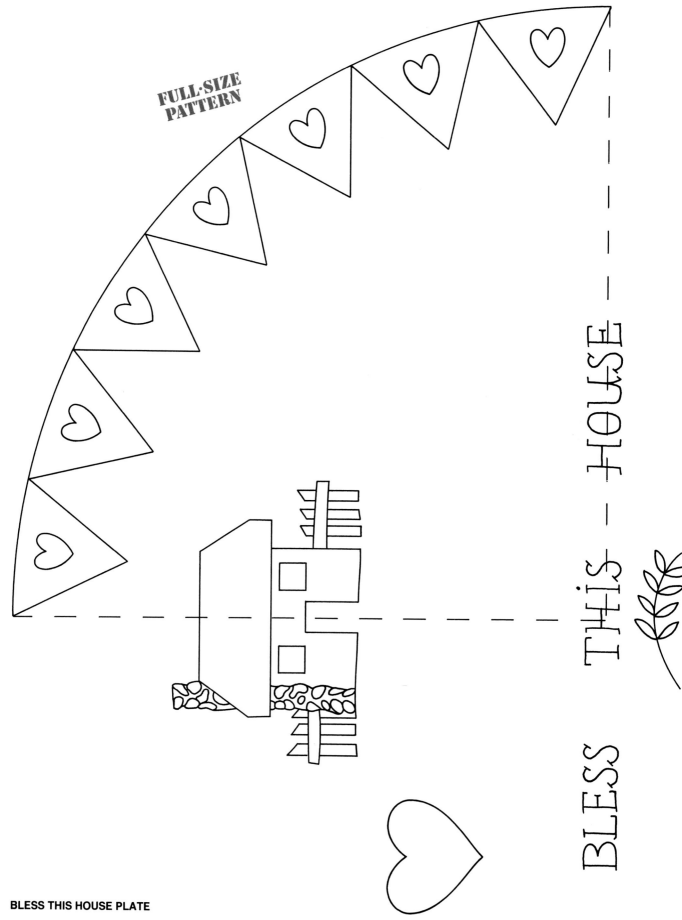

FULL-SIZE
PATTERN

BLESS THIS HOUSE

BLESS THIS HOUSE PLATE

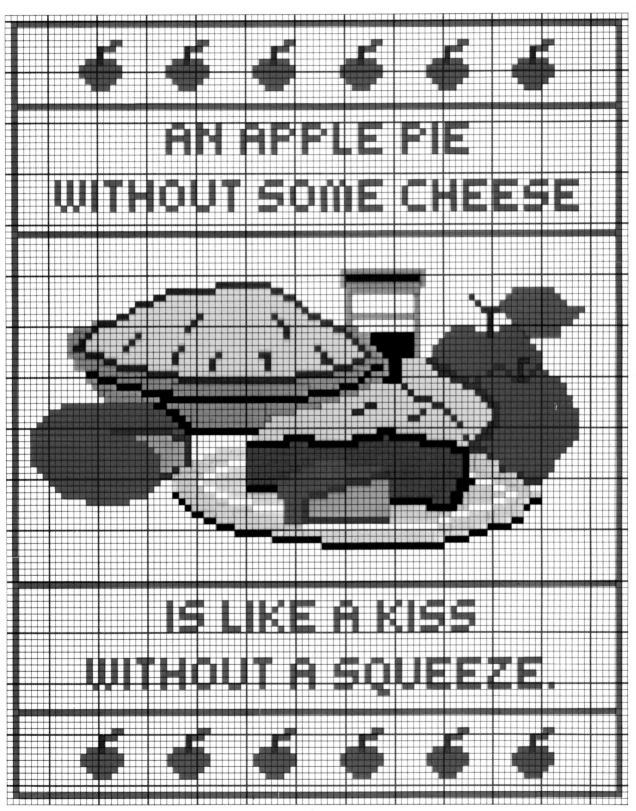

APPLE PIE SIGN

Apple Pie Sign

Shown on page 84.
Finished sign is 12¼x15¼ inches.

MATERIALS

1x11¾x14-inch piece of pine or an 11¾x14-inch purchased plaque
Sandpaper
Tracing paper
Graph and carbon papers
White latex paint
Flat paintbrush
Red, cobalt blue, white, yellow, yellow ocher, raw sienna, black, dark green, and orange acrylic paints
No. 4 round brush
Spray satin varnish

INSTRUCTIONS

Note: Paint should be the consistency of thick cream. To mix light colors, first place white paint in a dish, then add small amounts of color. Mix well after each addition. Continue to add paint until the desired color is reached. Test colors on white paper and allow them to dry before using (colors darken as they dry). When mixing colors, use your own judgment as to how much of each color to add.

Enlarge the pattern on page 93 onto a sheet of graph paper that is large enough to accommodate the full-size pattern.

Lightly sand the board and paint it with white latex that has been thinned with water. The natural color of the board will show through.

Use carbon paper to transfer the pattern onto the board.

Note: Refer to the photograph on page 84 for further details while painting. All objects are painted as if they are on a grid. This gives the board a cross-stitched appearance.

Paint the green outline borders with dark green.

Paint the apples in the top and bottom border rectangles with red, the stems with yellow ocher, and the leaves with dark green.

Add two or three drops of white to yellow ocher and paint the top of the piecrust. Paint the outline of the large apple, the outline of the crust of the pie, and the cut edge of the cheese with raw sienna.

Paint the lettering, apples, and the outside of the cheese with red.

Use orange to paint the inside of the cheese.

Paint the inside of the pie, the vents in the crust, and the stems on the large apples with yellow ocher.

Add two or three drops of cobalt blue to white and paint the plate. Add two or three drops of white to cobalt blue and paint the outside edge of the plate, the pie plate, and the cheese grater handle.

Add one or two drops of white to cobalt blue and paint the base, the edge under the rim of the pie plate, and the center of the handle of the cheese grater.

Use dark green to paint the leaf on the large apple.

Add two or three drops of black to raw sienna and paint the grater.

Allow all the paint to dry thoroughly, then spray the sign with satin varnish.

Watermelon Sign

Shown on page 84.
Finished size is 11¼x18 inches.

MATERIALS

1x11¼x18-inch pine board
Sandpaper
Graph and carbon papers
White latex paint; paintbrush
Spray varnish
Red, white, dark green, yellow, blue, and black acrylic paints
Nos. 3 and 8 round watercolor brushes

INSTRUCTIONS

Note: Paint should be the consistency of thick cream. To mix light colors, first place white paint in a dish, then add small amounts of color. Mix well after each addition. Continue to add paint until the desired color is reached. Test colors on white paper and allow them to dry before using (colors darken as they dry). When mixing colors, use your own judgment as to how much of each color to add.

Enlarge the pattern, *opposite,* onto graph paper. Use carbon paper to transfer outline to board. Cut out the shape with jigsaw. Sand board and paint all sides with a coat of white latex paint that has been thinned with water.

Transfer details of the pattern to the board with carbon paper.

Note: When painting, refer to the photograph on page 84 for details.

Begin by mixing white acrylic paint with one or two drops of red paint to create the desired pink for the background.

Paint the background *light pink.* Add another one or two drops of red paint to the light pink, creating a darker pink mixture to paint the center of the watermelon and the lettering at the top and bottom of the sign.

Paint the red end of the melon and the red checkerboard squares at the base of the melon with the red paint.

Prepare a mixture of yellow and one or two drops of dark green. With this mixture, paint the rectangular border around the lettering at the top and bottom of the sign, the leaf, the center rind of the watermelon next to the pink slice, and the red end of the melon.

Add one or two drops of white paint to the dark green and paint the outside of the watermelon and the outside edge of the slice. Add a drop of yellow to this mixture and paint around the leaf and the vine.

Add one or two drops of blue paint to dark green and paint the striped markings on the outside of the watermelon.

Add one or two drops of white to blue and paint the fork and the dashed grid pattern in the light pink background. Add a drop or two of black to this mixture to paint the shaded side of the fork.

Paint the seeds black.

Allow all paint to dry thoroughly, then apply one or two coats of spray varnish.

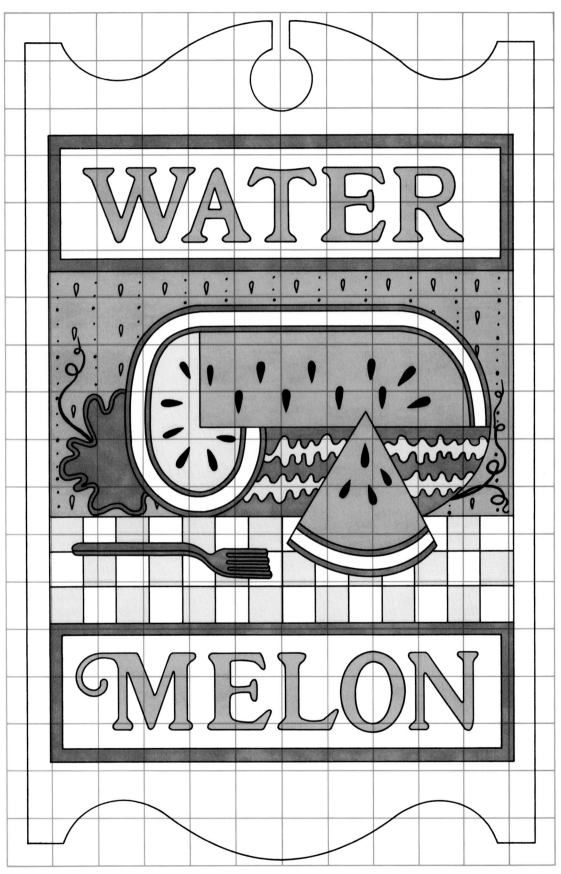

WATERMELON SIGN

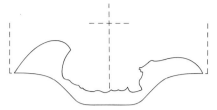

Stencil A

Stencil D

Stencil G

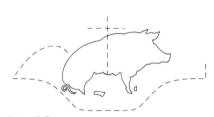

Stencil B

Stencil E

Stencil H

Stencil C

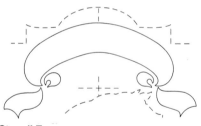

Stencil F

Stencil I

Pure Lard Sign

Shown on page 85.
Finished sign is 17x21 inches.

MATERIALS

Two 1x10x21-inch pieces of clear
    pine
Medium and fine sandpapers
Wood glue; router; jigsaw
Charcoal gray acrylic paint (base
    coat)
Medium gray acrylic paint (over-
    coat)
Old paintbrush with dry bristles
Paintbrush

Graph paper; masking tape
Chalk pencil; crafts or art knife
Wax stencil-cutting paper
Stencil brushes and stencil paints
    in the following widths and
    colors: 1-inch brush for ivory
    paint, ½-inch for rust, ¼-inch
    for brown, ½-inch for gold,
    ½-inch for yellow, ¼-inch for
    black, ½-inch for light rust, and
    ½-inch for brick red
Satin spray varnish (or water-base
    sealer)
Paste wax; soft cloth
Soft cloth (for wiping paste wax)

INSTRUCTIONS

Enlarge the pattern, *opposite,* onto
graph paper. Using your full pattern,
stencil-cutting paper, and a crafts
knife, mark and cut stencils A
through I, *above.* Mark the dashed
registration marks on each of the
stencils to assure their accurate
placement when beginning to paint.

PREPARING THE SIGNBOARD:
Join the two boards lengthwise with
wood glue to make a 20x21-inch
sign; let dry.

Transfer the outline of the full pattern onto the joined boards. Cut out
the sign shape with a jigsaw and
rout the edges all around. Sand all
surfaces of the board.

Seal the signboard (front and
back) with water-base sealer or satin varnish. Sand lightly if necessary.

—— **Stencil cutting lines**   — — **Registration marks**   **1 Square = 1 Inch**

Paint the board with two coats of charcoal. Paint over the dry base coat with medium gray paint using the drybrush technique (place very little paint on an old brush; stroke the brush across the surface so the bristle marks show on the wood). Wipe the edges of the board lightly with a soft cloth before the medium gray coat dries to make sure edges remain dark.

STENCILING THE SIGN: Mark the center registration lines on the board for stencil placement. *Note:* Outer edges of sign also serve as registration marks.

Place and tape Stencil A, matching the registration markings. Stencil lightly with gold. At the upper edge of the stencil, shade lightly with rust. Let paint dry slightly before lifting the stencil from the sign.

Place and tape Stencil B, matching registration marks; stencil yellow. Shade with rust at upper edge.

Place and tape Stencil C. Stencil mother pig in rust; with the stencil still in place, shade the pig with brown, referring to the photograph on page 85. While brown paint is still damp, shade *lightly* with black.

Place and tape Stencil D; stencil lightly with rust.

Place and tape Stencil E; stencil the feet black.

Place and tape Stencil F; stencil the banner ivory, allowing the trans-

parency of the light color over the dark gray sign coat to do the shading. Leave the ivory paint slightly thin and transparent near the banner gathers.

Place and tape Stencil G; stencil lettering rust.

Place and tape Stencil H; stencil the shading of the letters black.

Place and tape Stencil I; stencil both hearts with light rust. Shade the large heart with brick red.

FINISHING: Allow the sign to dry for 24 hours, then spray with two coats of varnish. Dry thoroughly. Apply two coats of paste wax and polish using a soft cloth.

GIFTS AND TOYS

◆

MY FAVORITE THINGS

Delight the children in your life with made-especially-for-you gifts from this collection. You'll find painted treasures to craft for youngsters of all ages—like the child-size chair and sweet pillow doll above, plus an arkful of animals, stenciled sweatshirts, and much, much more.

GIFTS AND TOYS

Every boy and girl will love this Grandma checkerboard, *left*.

Our Grandma is cut from sturdy ½-inch pine stock and quaintly painted on the back and front with bright acrylic paints. With her cheerful smile and ample checked apron, the old dear's a treasure to parents and kids alike, whether she's serving up cheese and crackers or a quick game of checkers.

The prancing reindeer and "I Love Country" sweatshirts, *below,* appeal to kids of all ages. The simple motifs are a cinch to stencil on purchased sweats, and you can easily adjust the designs to fit any size shirt. Just trace and cut out the full-size patterns on pages 120 and 121, or create your own designs using purchased stencils or original motifs.

Hint: Be sure to wash sweatshirts to remove all sizing before you start to stencil.

Gifts and Toys

These country-style versions of Goldilocks and her friends, the Three Bears, bring the old storybook tale to life once more for a new generation. Cut from sturdy pine and painted with durable acrylics, these simple jointed figures can take a lot of rough and tumble from younger children. They also make appealing collectibles for older kids.

Each doll is constructed of three pieces cut from 1-inch pine. The body, head, and arms are cut as a single piece, and the legs are each cut separately. The movable legs are suspended on lengths of coat hanger wire that are threaded through holes drilled in the sides of the bodies. This allows Goldi and the Bears to sit in any chair of their choice. The outline details are wood-burned on the front and back of each doll. Then the figures are painted with acrylics.

Directions and patterns for Goldilocks and the Bear family begin on page 121.

103

GIFTS AND TOYS

Hearts and flowers are prettily painted on the pull toy, *above,* and on the dainty doll vanity, *opposite.* Beside the vanity stand two plump little pillow dolls. Laura and Jennifer by name, these sweet-faced poppets are patterned after dolls of the Victorian era.

A perfect baby gift, the pull toy bunny moves along with a delightful rabbitlike hippity-hop, due to the off-center set of the back axle and the differing diameters of the front and back wheels. It's a simple, old-fashioned design, but one that delights toddlers.

For children who are just a little bit older, the painted vanity—or any piece of painted doll furniture—makes a very special gift.

Look for pieces similar to this one (with flat, uncarved surfaces) at crafts and hobby shops. The full-size heart and flower patterns on page 111 can be adapted to fit any size or shape piece (see the child's chair on page 99, where the same motifs are used in different configurations).

Easy to cut and stitch, the Victorian dolls, *opposite,* are drawn on muslin or canvas with a fine-tipped permanent marker, then colored with acrylic paint. Under simple frocks they wear painted shoes and pantaloons.

Instructions and patterns for both dolls begin on page 113.

GIFTS AND TOYS

Noah's Ark, a biblically oriented toy, was a popular Sabbath-day pastime for early American children who were expected to play quietly on Sundays.

Inspiration for this ark was drawn from an antique toy found in a midwestern farmhouse museum. The ark and animals are cut from ¾-inch pine, antiqued with a maple stain, and painted with acrylic paints.

In addition to Noah and his wife, there are 13 pairs of birds and animals, plus the one white dove that the old patriarch set off in search of dry land when the flood was over.

Part of the ark's charm—for adults, at least—is the quick and easy way it packs up when playtime is over. Both roof planks can be removed for fast loading and unloading of the animals (one roof plank is shown here doubling as a boarding ramp for the zebras). All the figures fit snugly inside the ark cabin, the ramp returns to its place on the roof, and the whole kit and caboodle can be toted away by its sturdy red handle.

Scale patterns for the ark and full-size patterns for all the figures appear in the instructions that begin on page 125.

GIFTS AND TOYS

For a one-of-a-kind gift the whole family can enjoy, create this colorful batch of wooden wickets to turn a store-bought set of balls and mallets into Barnyard Croquet.

There are seven different animals in the set—a spotted cow, a plump pink pig, a white rabbit, a silly goose, a turkey gobbler, a very proud rooster, and a snowy-white ram—plus a pair of bright red barns to mark the start and finish of the game. There are nine whimsical wickets in all.

Cut the basic shapes out of 1-inch pine with a jigsaw, paint the designs with durable latex enamel, and then draw in the outlines and details with permanent black marker.

Finish each piece with several coats of polyurethane for a long-lasting, high-gloss, all-weather finish.

Mounted on sharpened lengths of ⅜-inch dowel, these gaily painted wickets are easy for kids to set up, and easy for everyone to spot on the lawn. Patterns and instructions for the barnyard croquet wickets begin on page 129.

Painted Chair and Doll Vanity

Chair is shown on page 99; vanity is shown on page 105.

MATERIALS

Unfinished child's toys, such as chair and doll vanity
Masking tape
Tracing paper
Liquitex acrylic paints in the following colors: Titanium white, yellow oxide, venetian rose, and Hooker's green
Accent Country Color soldier blue
Fine sandpaper
Off-white primer paint
No. 5 round and No. 1 liner brush
Aluminum foil (for a palette)
Water-base varnish
Paintbrush for varnish
Dressmaker's carbon paper

INSTRUCTIONS

Lightly sand and prime the toys with off-white primer paint. Trim spools and edges with soldier blue paint, referring to the photograph on page 99 for ideas.

Trace the full-size motif designs, *opposite,* onto tracing paper. Using the design elements as desired, transfer the designs to the toys with dressmaker's carbon paper.

PAINTING THE DESIGNS: Mix medium pink and light pink by adding white to venetian rose. Paint small hearts with medium pink. Outline each heart with venetian rose.

Paint the large hearts with medium pink. Using the round brush, stroke a band of light pink around the outer edges, over the medium pink. Outline the heart with venetian rose. Dot the light pink band with yellow dots; let dry. Add blue dots to the center of the yellow dots.

For the leaves and stems, load the round brush with Hooker's green first, then pick up white on the tip. Paint leaves with single strokes, allowing streaks. Stroke leaves from the outer tip toward the stem.

For the tulips, load round brush with soldier blue, then pick up white on the tip. Paint the petals with single strokes from top to bottom.

For rosebuds, double-load brush with medium and light pink. Paint the bud with single strokes from tip to base, allowing streaks. Dot the tip with venetian rose. Add green sepals, painting them like leaves.

For the roses, begin with a circle of venetian rose. Add four venetian rose petals around the bottom. Side-swipe white onto one side of the brush. With white to the outside edge, make three petals across the top of the circle, restroke the four petals across the bottom, and stroke a small semicircle *inside* each of the four petals. Beginning at the top left edge of the petals, make an "S" shape through the circle with venetian rose and white on the tip of the brush. White should be at the top. Repeat the shape once more slightly to the left of the first.

Use the round brush to dot flowers of yellow with blue centers or venetian pink with yellow centers.

FINISHING: Coat the painted toys with three coats of water-base varnish, sanding lightly between coats.

Painted Hopping Bunny Pull Toy

Shown on page 104.
Finished pull toy is 10¼ inches high and 15 inches long.

MATERIALS
For the bunny
One 15x13x1¼-inch poplar board
6-inch-long piece of ⅜-inch-diameter wooden dowel
4½-inch-long piece of ½-inch-diameter conduit
Sandpaper; wood glue
Acrylic primer; jigsaw
Router with round over bit
½-inch and ⅜-inch drill bits
Four washers; small screw eye
4-foot cotton cable cord (size to fit through screw eye)
One macramé bead

For painting
Country Colors acrylic paints in the following colors: Painted desert (2300), stoneware blue (2440), apache red (2303), and barn red (2424)
Folk Art acrylic paints in the following colors: Tartan green (725), molasses (943), and lemon custard (735)
Apple Barrel acrylic paint in white (20503)
Folk Art water-base varnish, satin finish (792)
No. 4 round artist's brush
No. 1 round artist's brush
½-inch flat touch-up brush
Tracing and graphite papers
Graph paper

INSTRUCTIONS
PULL TOY ASSEMBLY: Enlarge bunny pattern on page 112 onto graph paper; make separate pattern for the two wheels. Use graphite paper to transfer patterns to wood. Draw four wheels onto the wood (two small, two large).

Use a jigsaw to cut out bunny and four wheels. Use a router with a round over bit to round and soften all edges.

Sand all wood surfaces to a smooth finish using several grades of sandpaper.

Use a ½-inch drill bit to drill holes through both front and back feet as marked on pattern (dowel placement). Use a ⅜-inch drill bit to drill holes ⅝ inch deep into each of the wheels as marked on pattern. The larger wheels are drilled off center so the bunny will hop when pulled.

Cut the conduit pipe and wooden dowel rod in half. The pieces of conduit now measure 2¼ inches long *each,* and the wooden dowels now measure 3 inches long. Insert a piece of conduit into each of the two feet (they should be snug) and insert a dowel into each of the two pieces of conduit. Pour a small amount of wood glue into the wheel holes and insert the dowels into the wheels. Place the large wheels at the back and the small wheels at the front.

continued

For small wheel on bunny toy

Bunny ear and front leg motif

CHAIR AND BUNNY MOTIFS

FULL-SIZE PATTERN

Mirror support

VANITY MOTIFS

Drawer

Center Fold

For large wheel on bunny toy

Borders

PAINTED CHAIR, DOLL VANITY AND BUNNY TOY

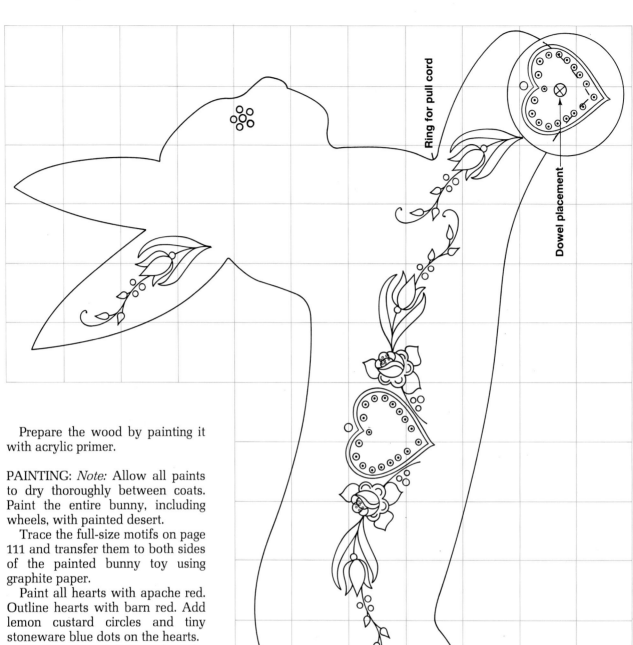

Prepare the wood by painting it with acrylic primer.

PAINTING: *Note:* Allow all paints to dry thoroughly between coats. Paint the entire bunny, including wheels, with painted desert.

Trace the full-size motifs on page 111 and transfer them to both sides of the painted bunny toy using graphite paper.

Paint all hearts with apache red. Outline hearts with barn red. Add lemon custard circles and tiny stoneware blue dots on the hearts.

For the leaves and stems, load the brush with tartan green, then pick up white on the tip. Paint stems with a single stroke, allowing streaks to form. Stroke the leaves from outer tip toward stem. Reload brush with green and pick up white as necessary. Dot the buds along the stems with apache red except on the ear. Dot the buds with lemon custard.

To paint the tulips, load the brush with stoneware blue and pick up white on the tip. Paint the petals with single strokes from top to bottom. Dot the bases of the tulips with stoneware blue.

Ring for pull cord

Dowel placement

Dowel placement

BUNNY PULL TOY

1 Square = 1 Inch

For each rose, paint a circle of apache red. Add four apache red petals around the bottom of each circle. Sideswipe white onto one side of the brush. With white to the outside edge, make three petals across the top of the circle, restroke the four petals across the bottom, and stroke a small semicircle *inside* each of the four petals. Beginning at the left edge of the top petals, make an "S" shape with apache red and white on the tip of the brush. White should be at the top. Repeat the "S" shape once more slightly to the left of the first. (Reverse the direction of the "S" shape on the rose to the left of the center heart by starting at the right edge of the top petals.) Finely dot white in the center of the upper three petals.

For the eye, dot the outer petals with stoneware blue and dot the center with lemon custard.

Allow paints to dry thoroughly. To create the stain, mix 2 tablespoons water-base varnish and two or three drops of molasses paint. Wipe on the stain with a soft cloth. Repeat if desired for a darker antique appearance.

Insert the small screw eye, centered ½ inch above front legs. Tie a 4-foot cord or braided ribbons to the screw eye. Push the bead over the end of the cord and tie an overhand knot at the end. Add a small amount of white glue to the cord beneath the knot, and move the bead up to the knot, covering the glue. Let dry.

Victorian Pillow Dolls
Shown on pages 99 and 105.
Dolls stand 16½ inches tall.

MATERIALS
For one doll
½ yard *each* of 100 percent cotton muslin for doll body and pastel print fabric for doll dress
⅔ yard of 1½-inch-wide ecru lace
⅔ yard of ⅛-inch-wide ribbon to match dress
⅔ yard of ⅛-inch-wide elastic

2⅔ yards of ¾-inch-wide white or ecru lace
Sewing thread; tracing paper
Polyester fiberfill
Additional dress trims as desired
Graph paper; tracing paper
Jo Sonja's acrylic paints in the following colors: Cool white, yellow oxide, rose pink, storm blue, burgundy, raw sienna, burnt sienna, brown earth, and carbon black
Jo Sonja's Textile Medium
No. 1 flat acrylic brush and liner for face detail
Dark brown permanent marker
Commercial palette

INSTRUCTIONS
The patterns on pages 114–116 include the fronts for two dolls and one back. The doll clothing patterns are on page 117. Select the doll front of your choice, then enlarge all patterns onto graph paper. Cut out all pieces *except* the two doll body (front and back) patterns. Trace the body patterns onto tracing paper. Tape the tracing to a window, then tape the muslin atop the pattern. Trace the doll lines onto muslin with a dark brown permanent marker.

PAINTING THE DOLLS: When placing paint on the palette, each puddle of paint should be mixed with the textile medium. Mix one part medium to two parts paint. When paint needs to be thinned, add water.

First add tiny amounts of red and yellow to white to make a flesh color. With the flat brush, paint eyes blue; paint small dot in eyes white. Mix raw sienna and burnt sienna, and use liner to line-work the nose. Base-paint the lips with burgundy and deepen separation line with brown. Lighten lower lip with pink.

Base-paint the face with the flesh mixture beginning at the forehead and working downward to bottom of eyes. Use liner brush and mixture of raw sienna and brown to stroke in the eyebrows. Pat line into flesh base to soften. With mixture of raw sienna and burnt sienna, stroke eyelashes and redefine the eyeline.

Complete the base painting of the face. To add cheeks, load the brush with flesh, side-load with pink, stroke brush on palette to blend the two colors together, and paint the cheeks.

Use liner and mixture of raw sienna and burnt sienna to paint in freckles while flesh paint is still wet. Tap freckles with a flat brush to soften their edges.

Continue to paint flesh in areas of neck and top half of body down to top of pantaloons.

Determine the hair color (black, brown, or yellow) you want for your doll. When the paint color is thinned with water, the color value will be lighter; when the paint color is thicker, the color value will be darker and more intense. As you paint the hair, leave a portion lighter on the top and a bit darker in the curls and separation lines.

For the pantaloons, base-paint the area with thinned white. Create the scalloped edging at the waist with strokes of paint by loading the brush with white and side-loading it with pink. Load the flat brush with white and side-load with pink to paint the flowers. For the leaves, mix yellow with blue. If you want to shade the pantaloons, thin down the blue-green paint and stroke it in the gather lines while the white base is still wet.

For the shoes, base-coat the area with an ecru-colored mixture of white and brown. Load brush with base color and side-load with brown to shade along the scalloped edge and toes. Dip brush in thinned brown and touch in the buttons.

BACK SIDE OF DOLL: Repeat the directions for painting the front side of the doll, except do not add the facial details.

HEAT-SETTING PAINTED DOLLS: When paints are dry, set iron at the designated temperature for cotton fabrics. Place paper toweling over the painted fabrics and iron both sides for 10 to 15 seconds.

continued

VICTORIAN PILLOW DOLL - FRONT

1 Square = 1 Inch

VICTORIAN PILLOW DOLL - BACK

1 Square = 1 Inch

115

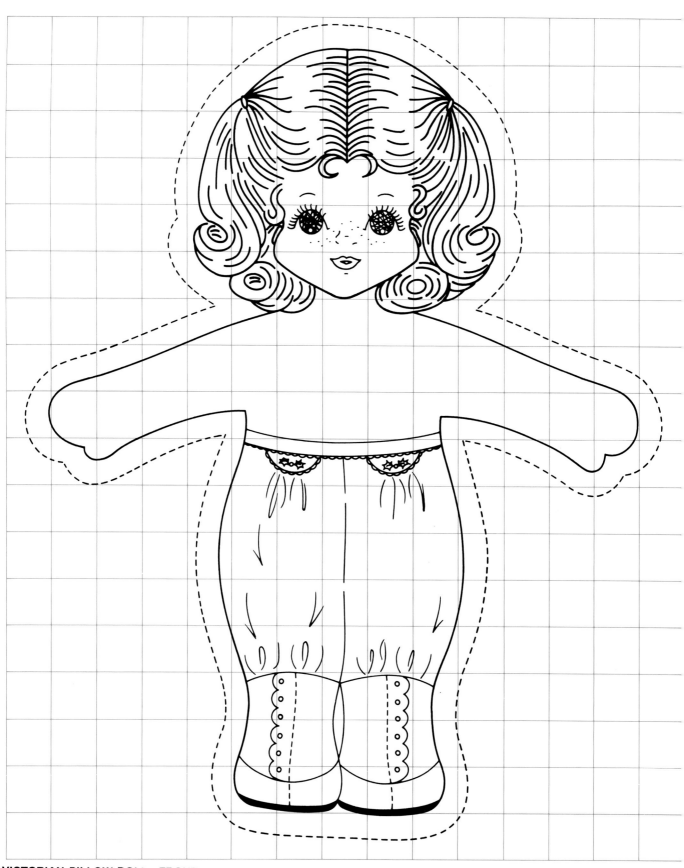

VICTORIAN PILLOW DOLL - FRONT

1 Square = 1 Inch

DOLL ASSEMBLY: Cut out the two doll pieces allowing ¼-inch seams. Sew doll front to back, right sides facing, leaving an opening for turning. Clip curves and turn doll right side out. Stuff doll with fiberfill and sew the opening closed.

Gather the 1½-inch-wide ecru lace to measure 13 inches and center it onto the ⅛-inch-wide ribbon. There will be 5½-inch ribbon ties at both ends. Hand-sew the lace around the doll body at the bottom of the pantaloon just above the shoes; tie the ribbon at the back.

CLOTHING: Pattern pieces include ¼-inch seam allowances. Sew all seams with right sides facing. Clip all curved seam allowances after stitching.

Cut pattern pieces from dress fabric. Sew sleeves to dress front and back. Press the fabric under twice along the neck casing line; stitch, leaving an opening for inserting elastic. Make ½-inch-wide sleeve casings as for neck casing. Trim the neck and sleeve edges with ¾-inch-wide lace. Insert 8 inches of elastic into the neck edge and stitch the elastic ends together; sew the opening closed. Insert 3 inches of elastic through each sleeve casing, securing the ends at the raw edges. Sew the underarm and side seams. Trim the dress hem with lace and ribbon, adding additional trims as desired.

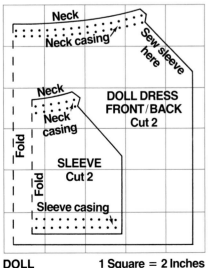

DOLL CLOTHING 1 Square = 2 Inches

GRANDMA CHECKERBOARD-FRONT 1 Square = 1 Inch

117

GRANDMA CHECKERBOARD - BACK　　　　　1 Square = 1 Inch

Grandma Checkerboard

Shown on page 100.
Finished board is 21 inches tall.

MATERIALS
10x22-inch piece of ½-inch pine
White primer paint
Acrylic water-base varnish
Acrylic paints in the following
   colors: Flesh, white, tan, light
   brown, dark brown, light gray,
   medium gray, pink, cobalt blue,
   royal blue, light blue, medium
   teal, dark teal, red, maroon, light
   taupe, medium taupe, cream,
   yellow, green, and black
Brown fine-tip permanent marker
No. 1 round, Nos. 3, 5, and 8 flat,
   and fine liner brushes
Fine sandpaper
Tissue paper
Graphite paper
Ballpoint pen
Dark and light buttons (playing
   pieces for checkers game)
Jigsaw; drill

INSTRUCTIONS
Trace the grandma doll designs on
page 117 (front) and *left* (back) onto
tissue paper. Transfer the doll front
outline to the pine board using carbon paper and a ballpoint pen. Cut
out shape with jigsaw.

Drill a small hole in the back for
hanging the doll on a nail, if desired.
Sand all surfaces smooth. Prime all
surfaces of the board with white
primer paint and allow the board to
completely dry.

Use graphite paper to transfer the
front and back details of the doll
onto the cut board.

PAINTING THE DOLL FRONT: Beginning at the top, base-paint the
outer hat light brown. Paint the inner hat dark brown and the hatband
medium teal. Detail the hat's texture
with cream. Dot royal blue flowers
with yellow centers across the hatband and add green single-stroke
leaves.

Then base-paint the face and
arms flesh. Paint the hair medium
gray and the neck tan; let dry. Re-

trace the face, hand, and neckline detail. Paint the eyes cobalt blue, the cheeks, mouth, and neckline detail pink, and the eye creases and nostrils tan. Use the brown marker to draw eyeglasses. Paint each glasses lens with a glaze of diluted cream paint. Paint the details of the hand and eyebrows medium gray.

Next, base-paint the blouse maroon, the apron cream, and the dress royal blue; let dry. Retrace the blouse and apron detail. Paint alternating apron checks and alternating apron bib border triangles cobalt blue. Paint the remaining border triangles medium teal. Paint the apron bib border stripe red and add red dots to the skirt. Paint the blouse collar and cuffs white. Dry-brush a narrow band of white just above the cuffs and below the collar; dot with white to create a lacy effect. Make black dot buttons on the blouse.

Base-paint the shoes light gray; let dry. Retrace the shoe detail. Paint the left sock (as it faces you) medium teal and the right sock dark teal. Paint the toe of the right shoe medium gray. Next, paint the left shoe top (omitting the laced area) light taupe and the right shoe top medium taupe. Detail the line between the left shoe top and toe with medium gray. Repeat for the right shoe using light gray. Paint the shoe tongues pink. Detail the shoe top and draw laces with the brown marker.

PAINTING THE DOLL BACK: *Note:* Paint the ½-inch edges while painting the back connecting the lines of the design.

Base-paint the hat light brown and let dry. Paint the hatband medium teal. Add texture detail to the hat with cream.

Paint the arms with flesh and let dry. Dot pink dimples at the elbows.

Base-paint the blouse maroon and the skirt royal blue; let dry. Paint the blouse collar and cuffs as for the front. Paint the apron ties cream and dot the skirt with red.

Paint the left sock medium teal and the right sock dark teal. Paint the left shoe light taupe and the right shoe medium taupe. Next, paint the

left heel light brown and the right heel dark brown. Draw the back seam of the shoe with brown permanent marker.

FINISHING: Paint the lower edge of the skirt white on each side of the shoes and let dry. Paint light blue wavy lines atop the white for a petticoat effect. Coat all surfaces with acrylic varnish; let dry.

Stenciled Sweatshirts
Shown on pages 100 and 101.

MATERIALS
For one sweatshirt
One 12x18-inch piece of stencil acetate
Crafts knife
Blue water-soluble pen
Black ultrafine-tip permanent marker
Masking tape; tracing paper
One ½-inch stencil brush for each color
Old cutting board
¼-inch-thick piece of glass

For the reindeer sweatshirt
Purchased white sweatshirt
Fabric stencil dye in the following colors: Dark green, dark brown, maroon, and slate blue

For the "I Love Country" sweatshirt
Purchased bright yellow sweatshirt
Fabric stencil dye in the following colors: Black, dark brown, red, and white

INSTRUCTIONS
GENERAL INSTRUCTIONS: Begin your stenciling projects by tracing the full pattern onto tracing paper with a fine-point marker. Secure the tracing with tape to a flat work surface. Then position and tape a piece of acetate over the tracing, and trace the outline of the stenciled area that will be cut away.

When a design requires more than one cut stencil, always trace the cutting line for one stencil pattern on the acetate with *solid lines* and the surrounding design with

dashed lines (registration marks). The dashed lines serve as guides and ensure accuracy when you position successive stencil patterns atop previously stenciled areas.

Label each acetate stencil (first, second, and third), to designate the sequence of stenciling steps as noted in the directions.

Lay the acetate atop a cutting board and cut out the design with the crafts knife. Allow a 1-inch border around the edges of each stencil.

Wash the sweatshirt to remove sizing. Draw a line vertically down the center front of the sweatshirt with a water-soluble pen.

When painting, allow each color to dry before applying the next one.

For the reindeer sweatshirt
Referring to the pattern on page 120, trace the full-size motifs and registration marks; then cut the stencil patterns as follows:

Stencil 1: Cut a 6-inch length of the sawtooth border, cutting every other sawtooth. In addition, cut a 6-inch length of the checkerboard border (the top line only) at the same distance from the sawtooth border as on the pattern.

Stencil 2: Cut three reindeer and the three small hearts.

Stencil 3: Cut three sets of basket diagonal slits *in one direction only* and three small tulips.

Stencil 4: Cut the remaining basket diagonal slits in the opposite direction and three sets of tulip leaves and stems, and diamond tulip tips.

Stencil 5: Cut three large hearts and three horizontal stem and leaf motifs.

Stencil 6: Cut two dots.

STENCILING THE SHIRT: Tape Stencil 1 to sweatshirt so the sawtooth border is on top, 3 inches below the neckband. Stencil both borders with green dye. Continue across the sweatshirt working outward from the center. When dry, move the sawtooth one tooth to the right or left and stencil the alternate ones. Next, turn the stencil upside down; paint another green sawtooth
continued

STENCILED SWEATSHIRTS

border 2¼ inches below the checkerboard border and stencil the second row of checkerboard.

Using your traced pattern as a guide, complete the remainder of the sweatshirt front with the cut stencils as follows: Stencil 2, dye reindeer brown and hearts maroon. Stencil 3, dye baskets brown and tulips blue. Stencil 4, dye baskets brown and stems, leaves, and tulip tips green.

Stencil 5, dye hearts maroon and horizontal stems and leaves brown. Stencil 6, dye dots blue.

Repeat the entire stenciling procedure on the sweatshirt back.

Mark the center of each sleeve and connect the front and back borders in straight lines across the sleeves with the water-soluble pen. Stencil the green borders onto the sleeves using the pen lines as guides. Stencil the sleeves following the directions for the front and back, working from center outward.

For the "I Love Country" sweatshirt

Referring to the design, *above,* trace the motifs; add your own registration marks, then cut the stencil patterns as follows:

Stencil 1: Cut the top line of the checkerboard border.

Stencil 2: Cut one goose and the white areas (main body) of one cow.

Stencil 3: Cut one pig, goose's beak and legs, and cow's udder.

Stencil 4: Cut the letters and the Xs in the heart.

Stencil 5: Cut the squares and rectangles in the heart.

Stencil 6: Cut one cow's spots, eyes, hooves, and the goose's eye.

Tape Stencil 1 to the sweatshirt with the checkerboard running horizontally 7½ inches below the neckband. Stencil the checkerboard red. When dry, move the stencil one checkerboard to the right and stencil the alternate squares.

Using your traced pattern as a guide, complete the remainder of the sweatshirt front with the stencils as follows: Stencil 2, dye the goose and white areas of cow with white. Flop design and stencil the opposite side of the shirt. Stencil 3, dye all areas red and flop the design. Stencil 4, dye all areas brown. Stencil 5, dye all areas red. Stencil 6, dye all areas black and flop the design. Use Stencil 2 again to shade the geese brown around the edges. Then use Stencil 1 to make the checkerboard border above the saying.

Goldilocks and Three Bears

Shown on pages 102 and 103. Papa stands 10 inches tall; Mama stands 9 inches tall; Baby Bear and Goldilocks stand 8 inches tall.

MATERIALS
One 1x12x18-inch piece of clear pine
Graphite paper
Tissue paper
Medium-coarse sandpaper
Woodburning tool
Turpentine
Rags
Burnt umber oil-base paint
Acrylic paints in the following colors: Black, red, dark brown, medium brown, cream, navy blue, royal blue, white, gold, light pink, and medium pink.
No. 1 round, Nos. 3 and 5 flat brushes
Black fine-tip permanent marker
Wire cutters
Coat hanger wire
Drill
Drill bit, diameter slightly larger than coat hanger wire

continued

121

FULL-SIZE PATTERN

INSTRUCTIONS

Trace the full-size patterns on these two pages and on pages 124 and 125, flopping the tissue to complete the half patterns. Use the same leg pattern for both Mama and Papa Bear. Transfer the pattern shapes to the pine board using the graphite paper. Cut out the bodies and legs with a band saw. Drill holes *through* the legs. Then drill holes *through* the corresponding places on sides of the bodies; drill ¼-inch-deep holes in the inside of the center leg areas. Sand the edges of all pieces.

Transfer the details of the dolls using graphite paper. Wood-burn the outlines of the details of each piece; do not wood-burn the outside edges. Wood-burn the clothing detail around the side edges and the back of the Mama Bear and legs of Goldilocks, and around the side edges of all the body pieces.

continued

GOLDILOCKS

BABY BEAR

123

FULL-SIZE PATTERN

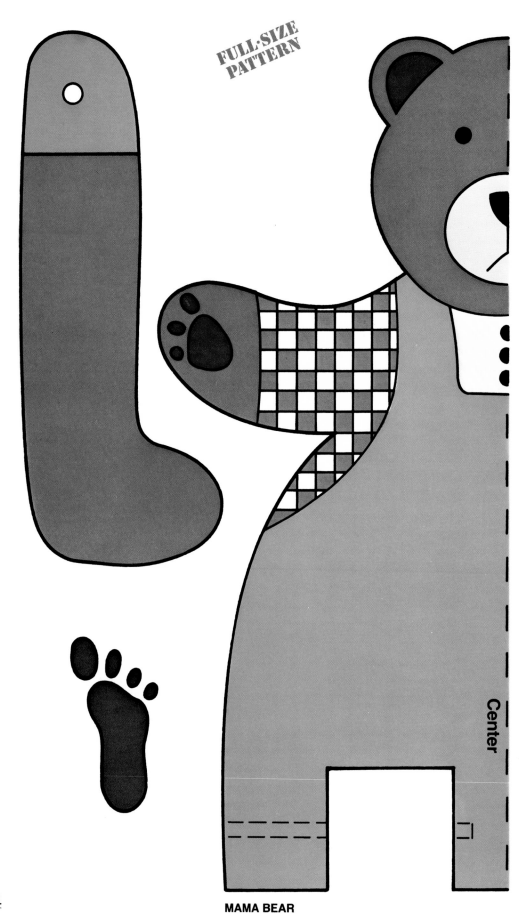

MAMA BEAR

FULL-SIZE PATTERN

Center

PAPA BEAR

PAINTING THE DOLLS: *Note:* The backs of our dolls are unpainted. You can wood-burn and paint details if desired.

Fill in the woodburned areas with acrylic paints; begin with the lighter colors and finish with the darker ones. Use the colors on the patterns as a guide. When the base colors are dry, outline the watch face numerals, chain detail, bears' eyes and noses, and Goldilocks' buttons with the black marker. Paint the paw print on the bottom of each of the bears' feet using the larger foot pattern for Papa and Mama and the smaller foot pattern for Baby. Paint Goldilocks' rosy cheeks and the dots on her dress.

FINISHING: When all painted surfaces are dry, lightly sand each doll to rub off bits of paint along the edges. To further enhance the antique effect, lightly brush on a coat of burnt umber oil-base paint. Rub the paint into all the wood surfaces with a rag saturated in turpentine. Wipe away the excess with a clean, soft rag.

Cut the wire into four 2½-inch lengths (for Mama and Papa) and four 1½-inch pieces (for Baby and Goldilocks). Attach the legs to the body by driving one wire through the outer body side, through the leg, and into the body center with a hammer. *Note:* Do not substitute nails for the coat hanger wire and drilled holes; using nails may cause the wood to split.

Noah's Ark

Shown on pages 106 and 107.
Finished ark is 8½x10x20 inches.

MATERIALS

¾x2x24-inch pine board for
    animal and Noah figures
7 feet of ½x8-inch pine
¾x¾x11-inch pine board for
    handle
Two ¾-inch pieces of 1-inch-
    diameter dowel for handle trim
continued

Four pieces of ⅜x⅜x2¼-inch pine
  for roof retaining strips
Two 5-inch pieces of ¾-inch-
  diameter dowel for ark end trim
Band saw
Maple stain; acrylic mat varnish
Graph and tissue papers
Sandpaper; wood glue
Nails
Graphite paper
5x7-inch piece of stencil acetate
Cardboard; crafts knife
Black and brown fine-tip
  permanent markers
¾-inch stencil brush
No. 1 round, Nos. 4 and 8 flat
  brushes
Latex enamel paints in the
  following colors: Red, blue, and
  black for the ark
Acrylic white, light pink, yellow,
  gold, orange, red, tan, brown,
  gray, slate blue, light green, and
  black paints for animals and
  Noah and his wife

INSTRUCTIONS

Enlarge the ark and cabin patterns,
above right, onto graph paper; cut
out. Draw shapes onto the ½-inch
pine for two ark sides and two cabin
ends; cut out. Also cut from the ½-
inch board one 5x15-inch ark bottom, two 2⅞x7¼-inch cabin sides,
two 4⅞x10½-inch cabin roofs, and
two 4x5-inch ark ends.

ARK: Bevel one long side of each
ark endpiece and each short side of
the ark bottom piece, joining beveled edges. Cut a 90-degree wedge
lengthwise into each ¾-inch-diame-
ter dowel with one cut side ½ inch
deep and the other cut side ⅜ inch
deep. Glue one dowel to each ark
end, matching the ½-inch cut side to
the leading edge of the ark end.

CABIN: Glue a cabin endpiece 2¼
inches in from each end of the ark.
  Bevel one short side of each cabin
sidepiece 45 degrees. Glue each cabin sidepiece, beveled edge up and
facing out, to the ark side and cabin
end as shown in the photograph on
pages 106 and 107 (there will be a 3-
inch space between the cabin side-
pieces on each side of the ark). Sand

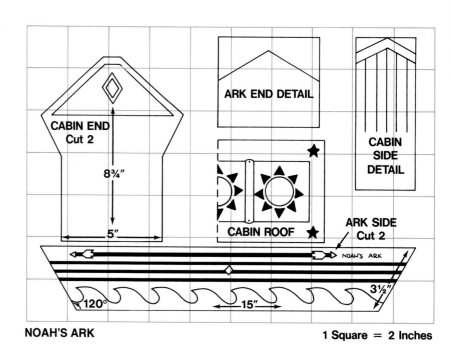

NOAH'S ARK

ARK END DETAIL

CABIN END
Cut 2

8¾"

5"

CABIN ROOF

CABIN SIDE DETAIL

ARK SIDE
Cut 2

NOAH'S ARK

120°

15"

3½"

1 Square = 2 Inches

FULL-SIZE PATTERN

STENCIL PATTERNS

126

the top of each cabin side level with the adjoining cabin end.

Center the handle over the end-pieces; glue and nail. Cut a 90-degree wedge lengthwise into each 1-inch-diameter dowel with one cut side ½ inch deep and the other cut side ¾ inch deep. Glue dowels to handle ends, matching the ¾-inch cut side to the vertical face of each handle, matching the dowel curve.

continued

FULL·SIZE PATTERN

NOAH'S ARK

127

FULL·SIZE PATTERN

NOAH'S ARK

Bevel one long side of each cabin roof piece 45 degrees. The beveled edge will be on the underside of the roof. Center two roof retaining strips 8 inches apart on the bottom of each roof piece, placing the short strip ends even with the beveled edge; glue all pieces together.

FINISHING: Sand all surfaces. Stain lightly with maple stain and resand. Transfer all painting detail *except* the sun, star, and animal silhouettes to the ark with graphite paper.

Paint red the handle, cabin end triangle, bottom section of each ark end, and the ark end trim. Using a small brush, also paint red the bottom two stripes, the top stripe, and arrows on the ark sides.

Paint blue the second stripe from the top, arrow feathers, and waves.

Use the brown marker to draw the roof, cabin side, and cabin end line detail and to print "NOAH'S ARK" on the ark side.

Trace the full-size sun, star, and animal silhouette patterns on page 126 onto acetate. Cut out with a crafts knife to make stencils. Using the ark pattern on page 126 as a placement guide, stencil red suns and blue stars onto the roof pieces. With slate blue, stencil an elephant silhouette onto two opposing cabin sides and a giraffe on the remaining two sides.

Sand all ark surfaces lightly to achieve a worn look. Apply a thin coat of varnish.

FIGURES: Trace the full-size patterns on page 127 and *opposite* onto tracing paper and cut out. Draw around the shapes on the ¾-inch pine; cut out with a band saw. Cut two of each animal except the dove. Cut one each of the dove, Noah, and Noah's wife. Sand each figure and paint as follows:

For Noah and his wife, paint the faces light pink, hair brown, and bodies slate blue. Paint Noah's hat red and his beard white. Draw the face details with the brown marker.

Paint the dove, sheep, and ostrich tails white, pigs and ostrich necks light pink, giraffes yellow, hippos and elephants light gray, camels and ostrich beaks gold, llamas tan, tigers orange, alligators light green, bears and raccoons brown, and the ostrich bodies and zebras black. Let paint dry, then add white stripes and tails on the zebras and brown spots on the giraffes. Draw the eyes and the remaining details on the figures with the black marker. Sand the figures lightly. Apply a thin coat of varnish.

Barnyard Croquet
Shown on pages 108 and 109.

MATERIALS
10-foot length of 1x12-inch pine
Eighteen 12-inch lengths of ⅜-inch-
    diameter dowel
White primer paint

continued

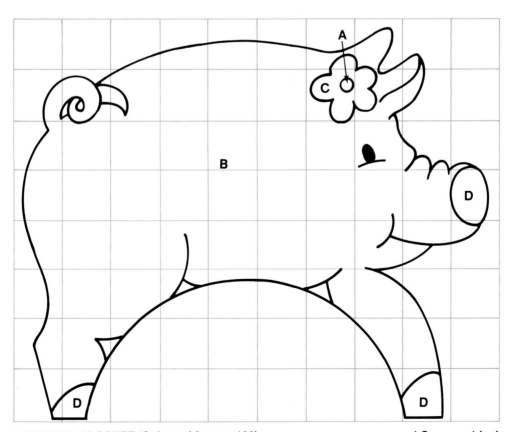

BARNYARD CROQUET (Color guide on p.133)   1 Square = 1 Inch

129

Latex enamel paint in the
    following colors: Yellow, pink,
    dark pink, red, gold, red-brown,
    light brown, brown, white,
    orange, black, tan, beige, purple,
    medium purple, lavender, and
    green.
Black fine-tip permanent marker
½-inch, 1-inch, and 2-inch-wide
    paintbrushes
Pencil sharpener
Polyurethane gloss varnish
Carbon paper
Sandpaper
Jigsaw; drill

INSTRUCTIONS

Enlarge the patterns, *below, opposite,* and on pages 132 and 133, onto graph paper and cut out. Draw around the patterns on the pine, placing each pattern perpendicular to the board's edge. Cut out shapes with jigsaw and sand all sides.

Drill a ⅜-inch-diameter hole 1 inch deep into both bottom ends of each shape. Sharpen one end of each dowel with a pencil sharpener and glue the other end into a drilled hole. *Note:* Dowels may be glued to the shapes after painting.

PAINTING THE ANIMALS: Paint all pieces with the white primer. When dry, transfer the painting detail to each shape using carbon paper. Following the letter codes on the patterns (see page 133 for letter codes), paint each piece. When the paint is dry, draw the outlining details and go over these markings with the black marker.

Complete the pieces with three coats of varnish, allowing each coat to dry before applying the next coat. Glue the dowels in place if you have not already done so.

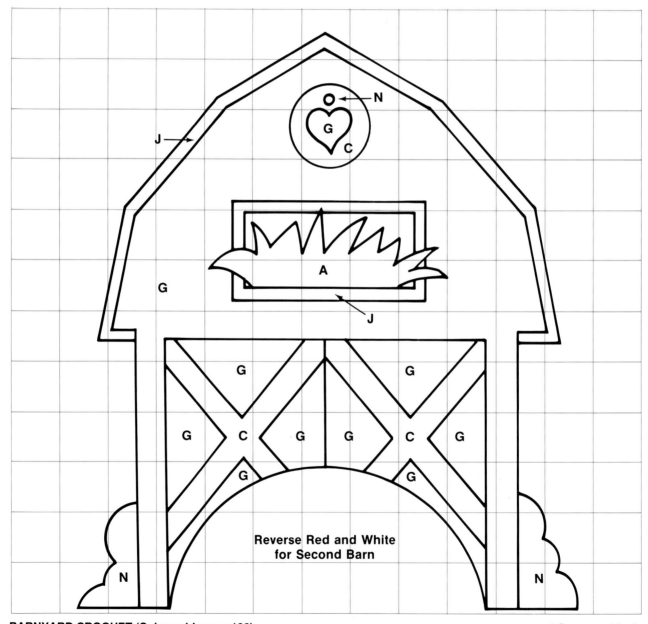

BARNYARD CROQUET (Color guide on p.133)

1 Square = 1 Inch

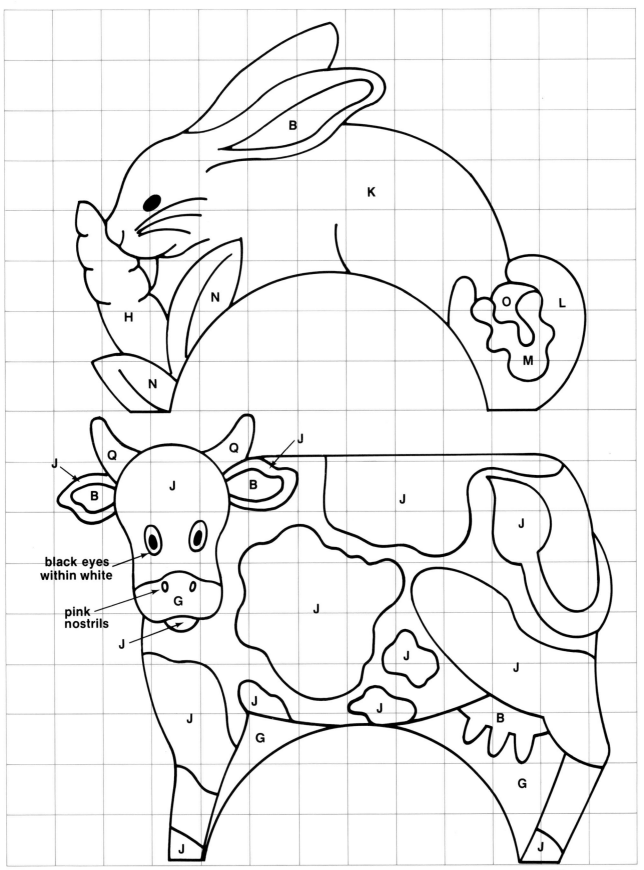

BARNYARD CROQUET (Color guide on p.133)

1 Square = 1 Inch

eyes
black
inside
white

BARNYARD CROQUET

1 Square = 1 Inch

purple dots on eggs →

BARNYARD CROQUET

1 Square = 1 Inch

A = Yellow   D = Dk Pink   F = Lt. Brown   I = Brown   K = Beige   N = Green
B = Pink   E = Gold   G = White   J = Black   L = Purple   O = Lavender
C = Red   P = Red-Brown   H = Orange   Q = Tan   M = Med. Purple

133

ELEGANT OLD-WORLD DESIGNS

◆

WHERE ROSES LINGER

Master the graceful motifs and age-old techniques of a truly distinctive folk art tradition: Norwegian rosemaling, or "rose painting." Full-size patterns and step-by-step instructions make it easy to re-create each of the old-world designs in this chapter.

ELEGANT OLD-WORLD DESIGNS

Rosemaling is a colorful and highly stylized form of decorative painting that developed in the rural areas of Norway during the first half of the eighteenth century. Featuring a whole lexicon of traditional floral motifs, these robust designs were used by artists to embellish all manner of home furnishings and accessories.

Early Norwegian rosemaling was markedly regional in style, and two different styles are represented in this chapter. The charger plate on page 135 and the cheesebox pictured here, *near left,* are both examples of the Rogaland style, characterized by symmetrical patterns, graceful tendrils, and circular designs.

The *tine* box (pronounced "tina" box), *far left,* is a traditional Scandinavian storage box painted in the Os style. Os designs are often asymmetrical, have thicker tendrils or scrolls, and frequently are painted freehand, rather than from traced patterns. Instructions for these projects begin on page 142.

ELEGANT OLD-WORLD DESIGNS

The delightful little dower trunk, *above* and *opposite,* is another example of the Os style of rosemaling. Although designs on the lid and on the front and back of the trunk are basically symmetrical, as in Rogaland style, these motifs have thicker scrolls and a more relaxed feeling that is characteristic of Os regional designs.

The trunk pictured here is 12 inches wide, 16 inches long, and 15 inches high. The domed lid and carved trim give it an old-fashioned heirloom look that is particularly appealing, but any trunk of similar size would be equally suitable for the pattern.

Whether the chest you choose is new or old, careful preparation of the piece is of the utmost importance. Fill any holes or nicks with wood filler, sand the piece well, then wipe with a tack cloth, and shellac to seal.

Once the background color has been applied (refer to instructions on page 147), trace the basic outlines of each design onto the painted surface and proceed to paint the individual motifs.

ELEGANT OLD-WORLD DESIGNS

An exceptionally lovely piece, this enchanting corner cupboard offers unique opportunities for imaginative embellishment. The lively, asymmetrical scrolls on both the inner and outer panels of the door, the casual shading on leaves and blossoms, and the inclusion of the cheerful yellow church on the front door panel are all quite typical of the Os painterly style of rosemaling, in which houses and churches were frequently integrated into the design.

Beautiful pieces such as these are sure to become cherished family heirlooms, and future generations will be pleased to discover whose hand wielded the brush.

Dates on the cupboard and trunk are quite prominent and incorporated into the design, but signatures should be added more unobtrusively—perhaps painted or penned (with indelible marker) on the bottom or the back of the piece. But wherever you choose to put your name, do be sure to sign every piece you make—or at least those you're really proud of!

Anno 1990

GENERAL INSTRUCTIONS FOR ROSEMALED PROJECTS

Introduction

One of the true folk arts, rosemaling, or "rose painting," originated in Norway around 1700. Most rosemaling originally was done by itinerant artists traveling through Norway working on commission. Hundreds of rosemaled items made their way to the United States with Norwegian immigrants. Today, both Norwegian and American artists continue to create beautiful examples of this traditional Scandinavian art.

Several rosemaling styles exist in Norway. In this chapter, the charger plate and cheesebox are painted in the Rogaland style. These designs are usually symmetrical and quite often use tulip variations and round flowers. Rogaland designs, while the instructions are more complicated, are easier for the novice to paint.

The *tine* box, cupboard, and trunk in this chapter are painted in the Os style. Os designs often include houses and churches. The scrolls end in tight spirals and the flowers are supported by thick stems.

Originally painted freehand, this style gives the artist a bit more freedom. The shading is casual, often using a color "borrowed" from a nearby area. Instructions for the Os pieces are more general, recognizing this more free and relaxed style.

Basic Supplies

Although rosemaling is quick and relatively simple, quality materials are essential to achieve the best results.

To work all the projects in this chapter, the following supplies are necessary:

Semigloss oil paints (for background painting) in the following colors: White, dark red, bittersweet red, medium gray-blue, and dark gray-blue.

Small tubes of artist's oil paints in the following colors: Prussian blue, phthalocyanine green, burnt umber, burnt sienna, raw umber, yellow ocher, cadmium red light, cadmium yellow, alizarine crimson, titanium white, and ivory black.

Shellac, semigloss varnish, paintbrushes for shellac and varnish, boiled linseed oil, brush cleaner, 8x10-inch

paper palette, flexible palette knife, fine sandpaper, chalk, tracing paper, pencil, cotton rags, and tack cloth.

Brushes are listed with the individual projects.

Preparation

Careful preparation of the piece you are going to paint is important. Fill any holes with wood filler and sand the piece smooth. Wipe the surfaces with the tack cloth and seal with shellac. Sand lightly and wipe with the tack cloth again. Paint the piece with the background colors and let dry.

Trace the desired patterns onto tracing paper. Using the side of the chalk, cover the back of the tracing. Lay the chalk side of the tracing on top of the area to be painted and go over the design lines with a pencil. This method creates chalk outlines of the design that are easily brushed away when the painting is finished.

Finishing

After painting, let the piece dry for one month. Brush away any remaining chalk lines and apply a protective coat of varnish.

Charger Plate

Shown on page 135.
Finished plate measures 14 inches in diameter.

MATERIALS

See Basic Supplies, *above*
Wooden plate measuring approximately 14 inches in diameter
Nos. 2 and 4 short artificial bristle brushes; red sable liner brush

INSTRUCTIONS

Prepare the plate for painting following the General Instructions, *above.* Paint the plate back and center front dark gray-blue and the border dark red. Following the Preparation instructions, *above,* transfer the design, *opposite,* to the plate front.

To obtain all the colors required for this project, mix the artist's oil paints as follows:

For dark green, mix equal parts burnt sienna and phthalocyanine green.

For medium green, add yellow ocher to the dark green.

For light green, mix yellow ocher with white; add a small amount of raw umber and cadmium yellow.

For medium yellow, add a small amount of raw umber to yellow ocher.

For light yellow, add a small amount of white to the light green mixture.

For dark blue, add burnt sienna to Prussian blue.

For medium blue, add white to the dark blue.

For light blue, add white to the medium blue.

For dark red, mix equal parts alizarine crimson and burnt umber.

For medium red, mix equal parts cadmium red light and burnt sienna.

For the middle white tone, mix white with a small amount of raw umber.

LEAVES: Thin paint as necessary with a mixture of equal parts boiled linseed oil and brush cleaner. Paint the leaves first. Stroke medium green down the center of each leaf with the No. 4 brush. Wipe the remaining paint off the brush; load with dark green. Apply the dark green along the straight sides of the leaves, blending the edges of the two greens. Wipe the greens from the brush; load one side with light yellow. Paint light yellow along the scalloped sides; blend. Load the liner brush with light yellow; paint the dark line along the scalloped sides. Add yellow vein lines.

FLOWER SEPALS: Paint the flower sepals going from dark to light green at the outer edge. Outline edges with light yellow.

CENTER FLOWER: Paint the inner half of the outer petals with dark red. Wipe off the brush; load with medium red and corner-load with light yellow. Paint the petals, turning the brush to give each petal a yellow edge. Blend the reds. Add more yellow to each petal edge and paint the turned edges of the petals.

With the No. 2 brush, apply raw umber to the base of each semicircle inner petal. Wipe off the brush; double-load with the middle white tone and white side by side. Paint the remainder of each petal with white at the outer edge; blend the dark and middle tones.

Double-load the No. 4 brush with dark and medium blue side by side. Paint the doughnut shape with dark

continued

Border

FULL-SIZE PATTERN

CHARGER PLATE

blue on the outer edge. Wipe off the brush; corner-load with light blue. Paint the shape once more to add light blue around the inner edge.

Load the brush with medium yellow and corner-load with raw umber. Paint the center circle, turning the brush to keep the raw umber at the outer edge.

TULIPS: Paint all flowers at the same time. Apply raw umber at the base of each center petal. Wipe off the brush; load with the middle white tone and corner-load with white. Paint the remaining half of these petals with white along the outer edges. Reload the brush with white; add scallop detail just inside the painted edge.

With dark red, paint the insides of the remaining petals. Apply dark red near the bottom of each petal. Wipe off the brush; double-load with medium red and light yellow side by side. Paint the rest of these petals in one continuous stroke, with yellow at the outer edge; blend.

Paint the lower part of each center raw umber. Wipe off the brush; double-load with medium yellow and light yellow side by side. With yellow at the outer edge, paint the remainder of each center; blend.

Apply dark red to the center of each of the outer petals. Wipe off the brush; double-load with medium red and light yellow side by side. Beginning at the base of the petals, lightly dot-brush the scalloped edge with yellow. Turn the brush over and paint the lower curve making a continuous yellow edge. Blend the reds in the center.

ROUND FLOWERS: With the No. 2 brush, paint the small outer petals like the center flower's white petals.

Apply dark blue to the inner three-fourths of the round inner petals. Corner-load the brush with light blue. Paint the remainder of the petals, turning the brush to give each petal a light blue edge. Load the No. 4 brush with medium red; corner-load with dark red. Paint centers of flowers, turning the brush to keep the dark red around the outer edge.

FINISHING: With the liner brush, add light yellow detail and embellishments. Begin with the heavier lines running from the center flower under the tulip sepals to the round flowers. Paint the cross-hatching working across the triangle shapes from each long side to the corner. Paint the smaller curved lines and the teardrops. Add the teardrops and dots to the flowers.

With light yellow, paint the border design with horizontal "S" strokes connected with short diagonal lines.

Stipple the plate rim by dabbing red colors from the palette over the dark red background paint.

Cheesebox

Shown on page 137.
Cheesebox measures 11¾ inches in diameter and 3½ inches deep.

MATERIALS
See the Basic Supplies listed on page 142
Wooden cheesebox
Nos. 2 and 4 short artificial bristle brushes; red sable liner brush

INSTRUCTIONS
Prepare the box for painting following the General Instructions on page 142. Paint the outer lid edge dark gray-blue and the remainder of the box medium gray-blue. Transfer the patterns, *opposite*, to the box lid and edge. Mix the artist's oil paints as follows:

For dark green, mix burnt sienna with a slightly smaller amount of phthalocyanine green.
For medium green, add yellow ocher to dark green.
For light green, add yellow ocher and a small amount of raw umber to white. If a brighter shade is desired, add cadmium yellow.
For medium yellow, mix yellow ocher, raw umber, and white; dull the mixture with a dab of black.
For light yellow, add white and cadmium yellow to medium yellow.
For dark blue, add burnt sienna to Prussian blue.

For medium blue, add white to dark blue, keeping the color soft.
For light blue, add white to medium blue.
For dark red, mix equal parts cadmium red light and burnt sienna.
For medium red, add white to dark red.
For the middle white tone, mix raw umber with white.

Thin the paint as necessary with a mixture of equal parts boiled linseed oil and brush cleaner.

LEAVES: Stroke medium green down the center of each leaf with the No. 4 brush. Wipe the paint off the brush; load with dark green and paint the dark green along the longer curved line, blending the edges of the two greens. Wipe off the brush; load one side with light yellow. Apply light yellow along the remaining side; blend.

Load the liner brush with light yellow; paint the shorter line along the side of each leaf. Add vein lines to the large leaves; paint the teardrop shapes.

FLOWER SEPALS: Paint the tulip flower sepals going from dark to light green at the outer edge.

SCROLLS: Paint the centers medium blue. Apply light blue next to the medium blue along the inner curve; blend. Wipe the light blue off the brush; apply dark blue along the outer curve and blend. When the paint is dry, detail each scroll using light blue on inner curves and black on outer curves.

CENTER FLOWER: Referring to the photo on page 137, paint the lower half of each outside petal raw umber. Wipe off the brush; load with the middle white tone and corner-load with white. Paint the petals, turning the brush to give each petal a thin white line around the outer edge. After all petals are painted, blend the shades using a circular stroke. Corner-load the brush with white again and paint the turned edges of the petals.

continued

FULL-SIZE PATTERN

CHEESEBOX   Lid Edge

Lid Top

145

FULL-SIZE
PATTERN

Lid

Side

TINE BOX AND TRUNK

Paint the inner petals, going from dark to light blue.

Load the No. 2 brush with medium red; corner-load with dark red. With dark red at the outer edge, paint the doughnut shape.

Dab light yellow in middle center circle; wipe off brush. Load with medium yellow, corner-load with raw umber. Apply the paint, turning the brush to keep the raw umber around the outside edge.

REMAINING FLOWERS: Paint the lower half of each round and scalloped petal in the same manner as the white petals for the center flower. Load the No. 2 brush with medium red, corner-load with dark red. With dark red at the outer edge, paint the doughnut shapes on alternating flowers. Using the same method as for the leaves, paint the side petals of the tulip flowers with shades of red and light yellow.

With the No. 4 brush, paint the lower one-third of each center with raw umber. Wipe off the brush; load with medium yellow, corner-load with light yellow. Keeping light yellow along the top edge, paint the flower centers.

FINISHING: Paint the remaining details and embellishments. Load the liner brush with black and paint all remaining lines and dots indicated on the pattern. Stroke from the design center to outer edge when possible. Paint a narrow red line around the perimeter of the lid top.

Beginning at the seam, paint the lid edge design with light yellow.

Tine Box

Shown on page 136.
Box measures 10½ inches in diameter and 9¾ inches high including handles.

MATERIALS

See the Basic Supplies listed on
   page 142
Wood *tine* or similar box
Nos. 4, 6, and 8 red sable flat
   brushes; liner brushes

INSTRUCTIONS

Prepare the box for painting following the General Instructions on page 142. Paint the box medium gray-blue with dark gray-blue handles and trim. Transfer the lid design, *top opposite,* to both sides of the lid top and the side design, *bottom opposite,* to each of the box sides.

Mix the artist's oil paints for this project as follows:
For blue, add burnt sienna and a small amount of white to Prussian blue.
For green, add burnt sienna and a small amount of yellow ocher to phthalocyanine green.
For red, mix burnt sienna with cadmium red light. Lighten with yellow ocher as desired.
For yellow, mix yellow ocher, raw umber, and white. Dull the yellow with a small amount of black.
Beginning with the lid, paint the large blue scrolls using the No. 8 brush. Paint each scroll with one long stroke. Paint the yellow scrolls with the No. 6 brush and the red scrolls with the No. 4 brush. Much of the desired blending is achieved by allowing painted edges to blend when a new color is applied.

Double-load the No. 6 brush with green and yellow side by side. Using as few strokes as possible, paint the green leaves. Reload the brush with yellow and paint the yellow leaves.

Paint the red flowers and the yellow flower parts and centers. Finally, paint the blue center of the middle flower.

When the paint is dry to touch, outline the scrolls, flowers, and leaves with black. Paint the remaining details black and light yellow.

For the sides of the box, paint the scrolls as for the lid. Add the yellow scallops, then paint the green and yellow leaves. Next paint the red flowers and yellow centers. Let the paint dry to touch before painting the black and yellow detail as for the lid.

Paint the red trim lines freehand just inside the edge of the lid and handles following the box shape.

Trunk

Shown on pages 138 and 139.
Trunk measures 12 inches wide,
15 inches tall, and 16 inches long.

MATERIALS

See the Basic Supplies listed on
   page 142
Wood trunk
Nos. 4, 6, and 8 red sable flat
   brushes; liner brushes

INSTRUCTIONS

Prepare the trunk for painting following the General Instructions on page 142. Paint the trunk bittersweet red with dark gray-blue trim. Transfer the oval pattern on page 148 to the top of the trunk lid and paint the oval dark gray-blue; let dry. Using the patterns *opposite,* transfer the lid design to the front and back of the sides of the trunk lid; transfer the side design to the base front, and transfer the rope and year pattern on page 148 around the blue oval. Transfer the corner detail to the lid at each of the four corners.

Mix the artist's oil paints for this project as follows:
For dark blue, add burnt sienna and a small amount of white to Prussian blue.
For light blue, add white to dark blue.
For green, mix yellow ocher with phthalocyanine green. Add burnt sienna to make the green very dull.
For medium yellow, mix raw umber and white.
For light yellow, add white to medium yellow.
Note: Refer to the photos on pages 138 and 139 when painting the trunk designs. While the *patterns* for the trunk are the same as for the *tine* box, the colors change and are different from those on the patterns.

Paint the scrolls on the lid designs dark blue, adding light blue along the inner curves. Paint the inner curve details light blue. Allow the painted edges to blend when a new color is applied. A motif may "borrow color" from another.

continued

FULL-SIZE PATTERN

Anne 1996

TRUNK

Corner

Lid

148

FULL-SIZE PATTERN

TRUNK　　　**Edge Trim**　　　Fold

Double-load the brush with green and blue side by side. Paint the leaves shaded green on the pattern using as few strokes as possible.

Double-load the brush with medium and light yellow side by side and paint the flower petals.

Paint the flower centers with a double load of green and blue, turning the brush in a circular motion.

When the paint is dry to touch, add the black corner details on the lid, the black floral design outlines and details, and the yellow flower dots with the liner brush.

Use the same brush technique and painting sequence for the front and back (side) design, adding yellow scallops when painting flowers.

Paint a ¼-inch-wide medium yellow border around the blue oval on the lid. Add the "Anno 1990" and curved detail using the liner brush and light yellow paint. Connect the black "S" strokes atop the yellow border to resemble a rope.

Using the edge trim pattern, *left,* paint the light yellow detail on the dark blue trim following the outline trim shape of the trunk.

Corner Cupboard

Shown on pages 140 and 141.
Cupboard measures 28 inches high,
21 inches wide, and 14 inches deep.

MATERIALS
See Basic Supplies listed on page 142
Wood corner cupboard similar in design to the one in the photograph on page 140
Nos. 6 and 8 red sable flat brushes; liner brushes

INSTRUCTIONS
Prepare the cupboard for painting following the General Instructions on page 142. Paint the inside of the door white. Referring to the pattern on pages 154 and 155, draw a rectangle the size of the design area. Paint the area beyond the rectangle medium gray-blue.

Paint the door front white. Referring to the pattern on pages 156 and 157, draw a rectangle the size of the design area. Paint a ½-inch-wide red border around this rectangle. Paint the remainder of the door front dark gray-blue. Paint the rest of the cupboard dark gray-blue with red trim, referring to the photos on pages 140 and 141 for trim ideas.

Transfer the floral design on page 150 to the front above the door and the "Anno 1990" pattern to the front below the door. Transfer the patterns on pages 151–153 to each side of the door opening. The three patterns on these pages combine to make one pattern. Overlap the designs along the shaded areas to make the full pattern piece. Overlap the patterns on pages 154 and 155 to make the pattern for the door back and transfer to the white rectangle. Repeat these instructions for the patterns on pages 156 and 157 for the door front.

DOOR BACK: Mix the artist's oil paints as follows:
For blue, mix burnt sienna with Prussian blue; add white.
For green, mix burnt sienna and yellow ocher with phthalocyanine green; add white.
For red-orange, mix burnt sienna and yellow ocher with cadmium red light; add white.
For yellow, mix raw umber with yellow ocher; add white.

Paint the large blue scrolls using one long stroke with the No. 8 brush. Paint the yellow scrolls and scallops and the red scrolls with the No. 6 brush. It is desirable to allow the painted edges to blend when a new color is applied.

Load the No. 6 brush with green. Using as few strokes as possible, paint the leaves and sepals shaded green on the pattern.

Paint the blue leaves and flower parts.

Blend a small amount of yellow into the leaves. Paint the yellow flower parts.

Paint the remaining unpainted areas red-orange.

continued

Top Front

FULL-SIZE PATTERN

Anno 1990

CUPBOARD

Bottom Front

When the colors are dry to touch, outline the scrolls in black with long strokes. Add the remaining embellishments using a variety of thick and thin brush strokes. The border consists of "S" strokes joined by short diagonal lines.

DOOR FRONT: Using the same colors as for the door back, paint the church yellow with a red-orange roof and blue windows. Paint the grass surrounding the church green.

For the remainder of the door front, refer to the patterns for the motif colors and paint as for the door back.

CUPBOARD FRONT: To obtain the colors required for the main part of the cupboard, mix the artist's oil paints as follows:

For blue, mix burnt sienna with Prussian blue; add a small amount of white.

For green, mix burnt sienna and yellow ocher with phthalocyanine green.

For red, blend burnt sienna with cadmium red light.

For yellow, mix raw umber with yellow ocher; add a small amount of white.

For the yellow detail, mix white, yellow ocher, and raw umber.

Paint the scrolls, leaves, and flowers of the top front design using the

same color sequence and technique as for the door designs. Repeat the procedure for the side front designs on each side of the door opening.

When the paint is dry to touch, outline the scrolls and leaves with black and paint the "Anno 1990" design using the liner brush. Paint the remaining detail black and yellow as desired.

Allow all painted areas to dry for one month. Make an antique glaze that consists of thinned yellow ocher with equal parts boiled linseed oil and brush cleaner. Brush this glaze over all surfaces; wipe off with a soft cloth following the direction of the wood grain.

150

FULL-SIZE PATTERN

CUPBOARD SIDE FRONT   **Bottom Portion**

151

CUPBOARD SIDE FRONT   **Center Portion**

CUPBOARD SIDE FRONT **Top Portion**

FULL-SIZE PATTERN

CUPBOARD INSIDE DOOR

Top Half

FULL-SIZE PATTERN

CUPBOARD DOOR FRONT

Top Half

JPBOARD DOOR FRONT

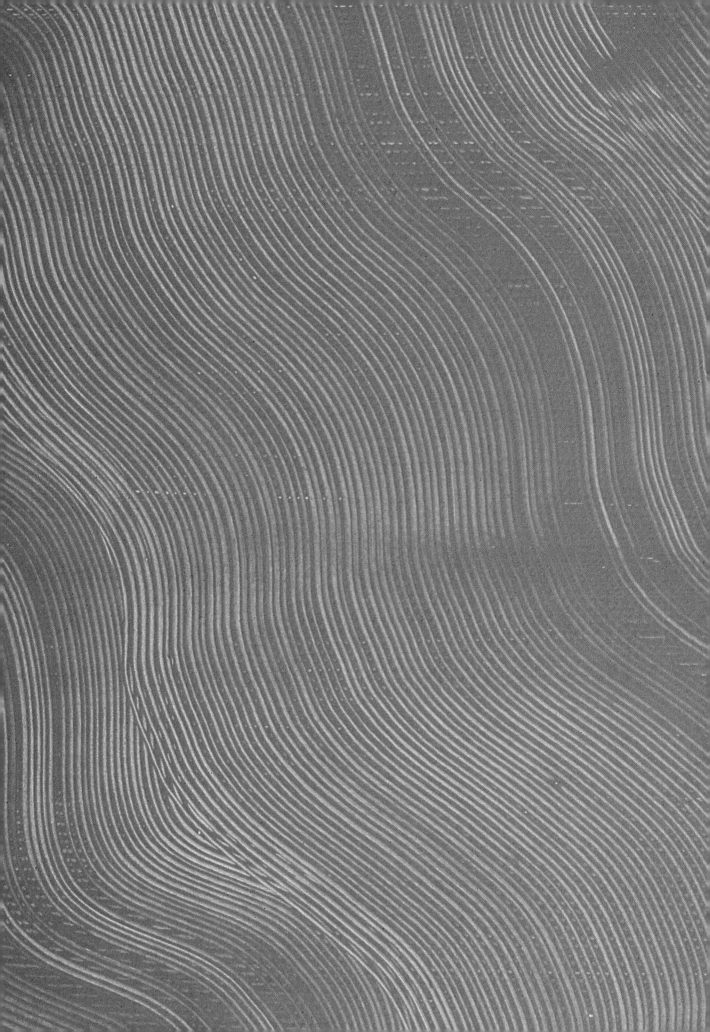

CHRISTMAS TREASURES

◆

A HOLIDAY FANTASY

Deck the halls and delight your family and friends with splendid holiday homemade crafts. Start your fanciful painting with the decorations, cards, and gifts you'll find in this chapter. Most are inspired by that much-loved song, The Twelve Days of Christmas, *and are adapted from the picture on page 161.*

CHRISTMAS TREASURES

Fraktur painting, practiced by Pennsylvania German artists from the eighteenth through the mid-nineteenth centuries, holds an honored place in the history of American arts.

Combining pictorial motifs and elaborate calligraphic inscriptions, these distinctive watercolor designs served both as records of important family events and celebrations—marriages and baptisms, for example—and as handsome decorations for the home.

Today, the term "fraktur" often is applied to any painted design that shows the same artful mix of text and illustration.

Many of the holiday treasures in this chapter, including the cards and tags on page 159, were inspired by this charming fraktur-style painting, *opposite*—a contemporary design that evokes that beloved old ballad, "The Twelve Days of Christmas," with grace and wit.

Below, for example, we've set the "seven swans a-swimming" around a wreath of pine and holly to create a most unusual centerpiece. Snipped from tin and sweetly painted on both back and front (they maintain their regal charm viewed from any angle), these swans are suitable any time of year. Nestle them on lemon leaves or in a wreath of dried flowers for spring. Instructions and patterns begin on page 168.

160

CHRISTMAS TREASURES

H ere are two ways to showcase motifs from the Christmas fraktur on page 161. Paint them individually on place cards and gift tags, *above,* or in mix-and-match combinations on a wooden stocking plaque, *opposite,* that's designed to dangle from mantel or doorfront to celebrate the season.

The plaque, cut from ¼-inch plywood and painted with bright acrylics, boasts wide, cheerful bands of pattern motifs, including geese a-laying, birds a-calling, partridges in their pear trees, swans off for a swim, a brood of French hens, and two pairs of dear turtle-doves. Painted ribbons neatly frame each band of motifs, and the stocking itself is trimmed with a matching fabric bow of red, green, and gold.

To create these cards and gift tags, trace single figures onto watercolor card stock. Then paint each design in acrylics or watercolors. Add messages using a fine-point pen. Instructions begin on page 173.

CHRISTMAS TREASURES

Motifs from the Christmas fraktur embellish these two gifts with an heirloom flavor.

The lighthearted design for the painted bench, *below,* pairs a dancing lady with a leaping lord.

They are entwined with a scattering of vines and blossoms. Figures and flowers are painted in soft, muted shades and lightly antiqued to enhance the old-fashioned aura of the design.

These same elements easily could be adapted for other furniture projects—a small tabletop or a chest of drawers, for example. Placement of the figures

and arrangement of the vines and flowers always can be modified to suit the available surface.

Demure turtledoves and a graceful bouquet of hearts and flowers ornament the face and decorative panel of the handsome wall clock, *opposite.* The clock itself is constructed from a ready-to-finish kit, available through mail-order sources (see instructions). But the

painted designs are adapations of elements from our Christmas fraktur. As on the bench, these designs are painted with fast-drying acrylics and antiqued with a mixture of oil paint, glazing medium, and turpentine. The colors, of course, can be altered to suit your own decor.

CHRISTMAS TREASURES

S traight off the pages of some imagined Victorian novel, these beautifully detailed figures come to life as eye-catching lawn ornaments. Customize these designs to suit your own family size. They'll make a splendid greeting for holiday visitors.

Ranging in height from 16 to 45 inches, the figures are cut from sturdy hardboard, sealed with latex primer, and painted with acrylics in a veritable banquet of colors. Details and accents are added with black permanent marker.

The figures are backed with sturdy hinged braces and protected with several coats of polyurethane varnish, ensuring that they'll be returning home for the holidays at your house for many years to come.

A partridge in a pear tree

Three French hens

Five gold rings

Seven swans a-swimming

Wi th twel da of Chris

TWELVE DAYS OF CHRISTMAS FRAKTUR

Two turtledoves

Four calling birds

Six geese a-laying

Eight maids a-milking

Top Right Quarter

Nine ladies dancing

Eleven Pipers Piping

Ten
lords
a~leaping

FULL-SIZE
PATTERN

Twelve
Drummers
Drumming

Twelve Days of Christmas Fraktur

Shown on page 161.
Painting measures 15x21 inches.

MATERIALS

15x21-inch cover stock style
  parchment paper
Grumbacher's designer's gouache
  in the following colors: Yellow
  ocher (YO), olive green (OG),
  Payne's gray (PG), burnt orange
  (BO), Naples yellow (NY), and
  white (W)
Pelican opaque paints in the
  following colors: Venetian red
  (VR), Indian red (IR), carmine
  (C), and umber (U)
Liner brush
No. 3 watercolor brush
Assorted calligraphy pens
Pelican black drawing ink
Tracing paper

Paint mixtures
NY + OG creates light green (LG)
W + PG creates light blue (LB)
W + a little more PG creates
  medium blue (MB)
PG + a touch of W creates dark
  blue (DB)
W + BO creates peach (P)
NY + W creates light yellow (LY)

INSTRUCTIONS

With a soft lead pencil, trace the
fraktur pattern on pages 168–171
onto tracing paper. The shaded areas on the patterns are for placement only; do not retrace them.
When the tracing is complete, cover
the lines on the *back* side of the tracing with a soft lead pencil. Lay the
tracing right side up on the parchment and carefully trace over the
pattern to transfer the design.

Note: Most motifs have at least
two colors. The first color is the
base, the second is the shading. The
shadings are along the outside
edges and the separations between
the objects. Refer to the photo on
page 161 as you paint.

With the exception of the leaves,
complete one picture segment at a
time before going to the next one.
Paint the border last.

LEAVES: Base-paint leaves LG and
shade with OG. Paint the stems U.

CENTER MOTIFS: Paint the hearts
BO and shade with VR. The first
petals of the outside flowers are
painted BO and shaded VR. The
second petals are painted NY and
shaded YO. The center petal is
painted VR, shaded with C. Paint
the two outside petals of the three-
petal flowers MB and shade with
DB. Paint the center petal NY and
shade it YO. Paint the spiral flower
petals LB and shade with MB. Add
three YO dots along the stem by the
blue spiral flowers.

Base-paint the body of the partridge in NY and shade the under-
body YO. Paint the wing and tail BO
and shade VR. Paint the head BO.
The top head feathers are BO, shaded with VR. Paint the pears LY and
shade with BO.

Base-paint the two turtledoves'
bodies NY and shade YO. Paint the
top of the wings BO next to the
head, NY in the center, and VR next
to the tail. Shade bottom of wings
VR, YO, and C. Paint one head
feather NY, shading the base with
YO. Paint the other head feather BO
and shade the base VR. Paint the
top tail feather BO and shade the
base VR. Paint the center tail feather NY and shade the base YO. Paint
the bottom tail feather VR and
shade the base C. Base-paint the
flowers with LY, and shade the tips
and base VR. Paint the two dots BO.

FRENCH HENS: Base-paint the
bodies with NY; shade with YO.
Paint the wings LB and shade MB.
Paint the heads MB and beaks YO.
Paint the combs IR and shade VR.
Paint the top tail feathers LB and
shade the bases with MB. Paint the
second tail feathers NY, shading the
bases with YO. Paint the third tail
feathers IR and shade the bases VR.
Paint the bottom tail feathers with
MB and shade the bases DB. Paint
the legs with U.

CALLING BIRDS: Base-paint the
bodies with LB and shade with MB.
Paint the wings MB and shade DB.

Paint the beaks NY; shade the bottom halves with YO. Using a liner
brush, paint a line of BO around the
beaks and at the separation. Paint
the top tail feathers NY and shade
the bases YO. Paint the middle tail
feathers IR and shade the bases VR.
Paint the bottom tail feathers MB
and shade the bases DB. Paint legs
with U.

GOLD RINGS: Base-paint the rings
NY and shade with BO.

GOOSE: Base-paint the body with
NY and shade BO. Paint the bow
BO and shade VR. Paint beak and
legs U.

SWAN: Use white to base-paint the
body and shade LB. Paint the water
MB and shade DB. Paint the beak
and the eye outline in U. Paint the
center of the eye YO.

MAID: Paint the face and hands P,
and the facial linework with VR.
Paint the hair in shades of U. Use LY
to paint the scarf and apron; shade
the folds with BO. Paint the blouse P
and shade BO. Paint the dress VR
and shade C. Paint the apron stripes
VR; shade with C. Paint the shoes
and bucket with shades of U.

LADY: Paint face and hands P. Fill
in facial linework with VR. Paint the
hair and shoes with shades of U.
Paint the blouse and the stockings
with LY, shade with BO. Paint the
dress LB and shade MB. Paint the
bands at the top and bottom of the
dress MB and shade DB. Paint the
stripe and dots in the band YO.
Paint the underside of the skirt NY
and shade YO. Paint the top flower
YO (shade BO) and BO (shade VR).
Paint two flowers with BO (shade
VR), VR (shade C), and NY (shade
YO). Paint remaining three flowers
and the butterfly YO (shade BO)
and P (shade BO).

LORD: Repeat colors used for the
lady to paint the lord and flowers.

PIPER AND DRUMMER: Refer to the photograph on page 161 to paint the piper and drummer. Paint faces and hands P. Use VR for the facial linework. Paint the hair NY and shade YO. Paint the red parts of the clothing IR and shade VR. Paint the pants and blue parts of the hats MB and shade DB. Paint the yellow parts of the clothing and the musical instruments LY and shade BO. Paint the shoes with shades of U.

BORDER AND LETTERING: Use a fine nib calligraphy pen and black ink to outline the border edging, squares, diamonds, and large lettering. Paint border, squares, and diamonds using YO and MB. Paint large lettering with MB and shade the lower half of each letter with DB.

Using a slightly wider nib pen, draw letters of small sayings.

Swan Table Wreath

Shown on page 160.
Finished size of each swan is 5¾x8 inches.

MATERIALS
Sheet of 6½x9-inch thin flat tin for *each* swan
Jo Sonja acrylic paints in the following colors: Warm white (WW), nimbus gray (NG), raw sienna (RS), Turner's yellow (TY), naphthol red light (NRL), raw umber (RU), sapphire (S), and carbon black (BK)
Retarder medium
No. 10 flat acrylic brush
Tin shears
Gray auto primer, available through auto parts stores
Satin spray varnish
Purchased wreath; holly; ¼-inch red ribbon; green floral clay
Tracing paper and pencil

Paint mixture
NG + S (ratio of 2:1) makes blue-green

INSTRUCTIONS
Note: There are seven swans to a wreath; both sides of each swan are painted in the same way.

PREPARATION: Trace the swan pattern on page 174 onto tracing paper; cut out the pattern. Draw around the shape onto the tin pieces to make seven swans. Use tin shears to cut out the swans. Prime both sides of the tin swans with the gray auto primer; let primer dry.

Cover the lines on the *back* side of the tracing with a soft lead pencil. Lay the tracing right side up on top of one tin swan and carefully trace over the pattern to transfer the details of the pattern to the tin; repeat for the remaining six swans. Turn the pattern over and repeat the tracings on the opposite side of each swan.

PAINTING: *Note:* Working smaller areas will keep the surface from drying out too quickly. Let paint dry before starting on wing and tail feather areas.

Base-paint the head (not the beak) and neck with WW, using overlapping "X" strokes. Paint head again with WW, then side-load the brush with the blue-green mixture and stroke the outside edge of the swan next to the beak. Continue working down the head and neck, painting with WW and side-loading with blue-green. A small amount of BK can add shading under the head and on the upper neck area.

Stroke WW thinned with water onto the back wing, stroking in from the outer edge. Stroke thinned WW onto the front wing, stroking in from the upper part of the outer edge. Then start at the front wing and stroke WW to the back and slightly downward. Paint the tail feathers the same as the wings.

To add shading to the wings, thin BK and stroke the thinned mixture into the wings; let paint dry.

Base-paint the beak and feet RS. Let paint dry.

Again base-paint RS in the beak area. Side-load the brush with RU and shade the area next to the head. While this area is still damp and RU is still on the brush, stroke in the shading on the bottom of the beak and the separation line. Rinse the brush, reload with RS and side-load with TY to lighten the front and top of the beak. Let paint dry.

Base-paint the feet again using RS and shade with RU. Lighten the front lower edge of the feet with TY.

Paint the oval-shaped eye BK and highlight it off-center with WW. Use a small flat brush and the blue-green mixture or BK shading and stroke around the eye with the shading next to the eye.

For the cheek, load the brush with WW, side-load with NRL. Stroke a half-moon shape with the red curve next to the eye.

Paint the opposite side of the swan and allow to dry. Paint all swans.

Use a satin spray varnish to finish all the swans.

WREATH CONSTRUCTION: Buy or make a wreath of live evergreen, adding sprigs of holly if desired. Tie red bows around necks of three swans. Lay the wreath on the table and alternate inserting plain and bow-tied swans into the wreath. Space the swans evenly around the wreath. The prong at the base of each swan will poke into the wreath to hold the swans upright. Use green floral clay to give the swans added support if necessary.

Gift Cards

Shown on pages 159 and 163.

MATERIALS
Off-white watercolor paper
Jo Sonja acrylic paints in the following colors: Burgundy (B), warm white (WW), yellow oxide (YO), raw sienna (RS), naphthol red light (NRL), green oxide (GO), pine green (PG), storm blue (SB), and carbon black (BK)
Nos. 0, 1, 2, and 4 acrylic brushes
10/0 liner brush
Paper palette or tray
Tracing paper, soft lead pencil
Fine-point permanent black marking pen
Spray fixative

continued

FULL·SIZE PATTERN

Paint mixtures

WW + YO + RS (ratio of 1:1:½) creates light yellow (LY)

NRL + YO + B (ratio of 1:1:touch of B) creates light red (LR)

NRL + RS + B (ratio of 1:1:1) creates dark red (DR)

INSTRUCTIONS

PREPARATION: Trace the designs of your choice using the patterns on pages 168–171 for the Twelve Days of Christmas Fraktur onto tracing paper. Color the *back side* of the tracing lines with a soft lead pencil.

Cut the card paper to desired size for either a folded or flat card. The shape of the card can be the same as the design from any of the fraktur plaque, but slightly larger. Lay the tracing right side up on the card paper and carefully trace over all lines to transfer the design to the water-color paper.

PAINTING: Follow the painting instructions for the four calling birds, three French hens, the swan, and the goose as given for the stocking plaque, *opposite*. For the piper and the drummer, repeat the red colors as outlined for them in the fraktur

SWAN TABLE WREATH

instructions on page 173, but replace the blue colors with the greens listed for these gift cards on page 173.

Paint a border around the cut card, and use a fine point or a calligraphy pen to letter the wording on each card or tag.

For the piper and the drummer, cut around the portion of the hat that sticks up beyond the border and then fold the card in half, letting the hat stand up above the fold.

Lightly spray the paintings with the fixative.

Stocking Plaque
Shown on page 162.
Finished stocking is 9x18½ inches.

MATERIALS
13x19x¼-inch plywood board
Jo Sonja acrylic paints in the following colors: Warm white (WW), yellow oxide (YO), raw sienna (RS), naphthol red light (NRL), burgundy (B), green oxide (GO), pine green (PG), and storm blue (SB)
Nos. 0, 2, 4, and 8 acrylic brushes
10/0 liner brush
Retarder medium
Paper palette or tray
Tracing paper; pencil
Acrylic wood sealer; sandpaper
Graph paper; graphite paper

Paint mixtures:
WW + YO + RS (ratio of 1:1:½) creates light yellow (LY)
NRL + YO + B (ratio of 1:1:touch) creates light red (LR)
NRL + RS + B (ratio of 1:1:1) creates dark red (DR)

INSTRUCTIONS
PREPARATION: Enlarge stocking pattern on page 176 onto graph paper; cut out pattern. Draw around stocking shape onto wood; cut out. Sand and seal wood stocking with acrylic sealer. Cover plaque with two coats of WW; let dry.

Use graphite paper to transfer the details of the pattern to the plaque.

Make a pale green mixture of WW and GO; paint a 1-inch-wide stripe around the edges; let dry.

PAINTING: Work with one color at a time. Paint the solid areas first; the *linework* (thinned paint used with liner brush) is stroked in after the objects are painted. A drop of retarder medium added to the paints will keep them from drying too fast.

CUFF: Base-paint the top and bottom cuff sections with two coats of GO, letting the paint dry between coats. Load the brush with GO and side-load in PG. Paint horizontal strokes on the band, laying the dark at top and bottom. For the ½-inch squares, base-paint two coats of alternating LR and WW. Outline LR squares with DR using the liner brush.

GEESE AND SWAN BORDERS: Load brush with WW and side-load with GO. Blend on palette to soften green into white to make a pale green. Stroke with the green to the outside or where there is shading. The beak and feet are base-painted with LY, shaded with RS. Bow is base-painted with LR and shaded with DR. Paint eyes with a dot of SB and highlight the center with WW.

CALLING BIRD BORDER: Stroke the bodies with GO. With LY, paint the beak, legs, and center tail feathers and shade with RS. The top tail feather is painted with a C-shape stroke using LR; the bottom feather is DR. Repeat GO on the body and shade the curve of the back with PG. To shade bottom of body, load the brush in GO, side-load in PG, and stroke out to sides from the legs.

PARTRIDGE BORDER: Paint and shade the body of the partridge with the same colors and techniques as the calling birds. The leaves are stroked with GO, shaded with PG. Paint the pear and all linework with LY and shade with RS.

FRENCH HEN BORDER: The bodies of the French hens are painted with the same colors and strokes as the calling birds. For the head and top and bottom feathers, use GO and shade with PG. The beak, legs, and second feathers from the top

are LY and shaded with RS. Paint the comb and third feather with LR and shade with DR.

TURTLEDOVE BORDER: Paint the dove bodies with the same colors as the partridge except that the stripe of LR is stroked over the dark wing area on the back of the doves. The heads, flowers, and head (back of head) and tail feathers (first and third) are base-painted LR and shaded DR. The front head feather and the middle tail feather are base-painted LY and shaded RS. Paint the leaves and stems the same as for the pear tree.

BORDER STRIPES: Paint the top stripe of the first set of dividing bands GO; then paint the diamonds LR, outlining them with DR. Paint the next stripe PG.

Paint the top stripe of the second set of dividing bands LR and the diamonds GO, outlined with PG. Paint the next stripe DR.

Alternate these two sets of dividing bands between the design rows. There are three dividing bands in each of the two color combinations.

Bench and Clock
Shown on pages 164 and 165.
Bench top is 36x14 inches.
The clock measures 20½x13½ inches and is 4 inches deep.

MATERIALS
For both projects
Off-white acrylic primer
Jo Sonja acrylic paints in the following colors: Warm white (WW), yellow oxide (YO), raw sienna (RS), burnt sienna (BS), naphthol red light (NRL), teal green (TG), burgundy (B), sapphire (S), green oxide (GO), and carbon black (BK)
Assorted flat artist's brushes
Retarder medium
10/0 liner brush
Paper palette or tray
Tracing paper; pencil
Graphite paper

continued

STOCKING PLAQUE

1 Square = 1 Inch

For the bench
Five-board bench (available from Bartley Collection, Ltd., 3 Airpark Dr., Easton, MD 21601)

For the clock
Wall clock kit, F322 (available through Shaker Workshops, P.O. Box 1028, Concord, MA 01742)

For antiquing, varnishing, and spattering
Liquitex oil paint in yellow ocher, raw sienna, and cerulean blue

Winsor Newton blending and glazing medium

Odorless turpentine

Satin-finish polyurethane spray varnish (petroleum base)

Large flat oil brush

Mop brush; soft cloth

Paint mixtures
Mixture 1: NRL + RS (ratio of 2:1) creates a dull red

Mixture 2: B + TG (ratio of 5:1) creates a dark red

Mixture 3: GO + NRL (ratio of 5:1) creates a dull green

Mixture 4: TG + B (ratio of 6:1) creates a dull dark green

Mixture 5: S + BK (ratio of 2:1) creates a dark dull blue

Mixture 6: WW + NRL + YO + S (ratio of 4:1:1:dot of S) creates a medium flesh

Mixture 7: WW + NRL + YO + S (same as above except less white) creates a dark flesh

INSTRUCTIONS
PREPARATION: Prepare bench top or clock front panel with acrylic primer. Trace the appropriate patterns onto tracing paper. Patterns for the bench are on pages 179–181; patterns for the clock are on page 182. The bench schematic drawing on page 178 is a guide for placement of designs to make a full pattern. Use graphite paper to transfer designs to the bench or clock.

Prepare paints and mixtures. A drop of retarder medium added to all paints will keep them moist on the palette as you work.

GENERAL INSTRUCTIONS: The term *linework* refers to a line of thinned paint drawn with the liner brush. The long linework, such as

stems in burnt sienna, is the first painting to be done. Using one color at a time, paint all the red motifs, then the blue, yellow, and finally the green. The short linework, or outlining, is painted last.

Some motifs require painting with a side-loaded brush. Without mixing the paints, work in a little water to soften the color. Stroke with the darker paint to the outside of the motifs, reducing paint coverage to nothing toward its center.

For each motif, paint all Step 1 applications as described. *Let paint dry between steps*, then paint Step 2 applications. All the leaves require three steps.

For the bench
RED FLOWERS AND CLOTHING: Side-load brush with Mixture 1. Blend on palette to soften color. Stroke along the outer edges when applying paint. With Mixture 2, repeat strokes and positioning of previous step.

BLUE CLOTHING, OUTSIDE BUTTERFLY WINGS, AND FLOWERS: Dip brush in water, then side-load with S. Blend on palette to soften color. Stroke inside edge of brush toward the stem for the flowers. Stroke outside edges for the clothing. With Mixture 5, repeat strokes and position of paint from the previous step.

YELLOW FLOWERS, CLOTHING, HEARTS, AND INSIDE BUTTERFLY WINGS: Dip brush in water, then side-load with YO. Blend on palette to soften color. Stroke color on the outer edges of the motifs.

Next, repeat all strokes as in the previous step, except use RS in place of YO.

Apply a wash of light yellow (water and a little paint) to all the yellow design areas. Then add a side load of RS. Stroke, placing the RS where it will shade or separate adjacent painted areas.

LEAVES: Dip brush in water, then side-load with YO and blend on palette to soften color. Paint leaf with an "S" stroke, starting at the tip.

Dip brush in water, then side-load with Mixture 3. Blend on palette, then paint lower half of leaf.

Dip brush in the retarder medium, then side-load with Mixture 4. Blend on palette to soften color. Paint bottom edge of leaf.

HANDS AND FACES: Use Mixture 6 to base-paint twice on the face, neck, and hands. Load brush with Mixture 6, then side-load with Mixture 7. Brush-stroke the face with Mixture 7 (dark) next to the hairline. Paint the neck with shading under the face. Stroke on the hands with shading next to the sleeve and by the fold of the fingers.

Base-paint the eyes with S. Paint pupils and eyelashes with BK. Highlight pupil with a dot of WW.

For the cheeks, load brush with Mixture 6; side-load with Mixture 1, and blend to soften. Stroke with darker color just below eyes.

Use liner brush and thinned BS to define nose and mouth. With tip of brush, touch in Mixture 1 in the peak areas of the upper lip.

HAIR: Dip brush in water, then side-load with YO. Blend on palette to soften color. Stroke brush upwards to outer edge of hair.

Next repeat the previous step except use RS. Also stroke in bangs.

SHOES AND BOOTS: Apply a light wash of BS to the shoes.

Next, load the brush with a BS wash and side-load with BS. Stroke, with BS placed for shading.

OUTLINES AND DETAILS: Use the liner brush and thinned BS to outline red flowers, blue scrolls, all the yellow objects, leaves, boots, and shoes. Add stems. Use the liner brush to add dots of B, YO, and S.

ANTIQUING: When painted surface is completely dry, apply a coat of spray polyurethane varnish. Let varnish dry. The varnish gives you better control of the antiquing. If the antiquing results are unsatisfactory, you can remove it right away without damaging the paint.

continued

BENCH SCHEMATIC

Mix yellow ocher and raw sienna oil paints in a 2:1 ratio; thin the paint mixture with the glazing medium.

Dip the large flat oil brush into a mixture of equal parts of glazing and turpentine. Dampen the bench top from the center outward. Using the same brush, pick up the glazing mixture and start brushing darker areas around the outside of the bench; lessen coverage of antiquing toward the middle.

Use the soft cloth to wipe off the antiquing, beginning in the center. Leave more antiquing along the outside edges. Soften the outside edges with a mop brush. Allow to dry.

VARNISHING AND SPATTERING: Apply one coat of the spray polyurethane varnish. Allow to dry. Cover the center and motifs with toweling so as not to spatter over them.

Make a mixture of cerulean blue thinned with odorless turpentine to the consistency of soft margarine and load the palette knife. To spatter, hold loaded knife horizontally and pull the brush over the edge. (Practice on another surface to get the feel of it.) Spatter background area of bench top. Allow to dry.

Spray on six coats of satin-finish polyurethane spray varnish, waiting 10 minutes between applications. Wait at least 48 hours before applying more coats of the polyurethane spray. Repeat the varnishing procedure until you have achieved the coverage desired.

For the clock
RED FLOWERS, HEARTS, BIRDS' WINGS AND BEAKS: Dip brush in water, then side-load with Mixture 1. Blend on palette to soften color. Stroke toward the outer edge.

Next, repeat strokes as in first step, except use Mixture 2.

BLUE FLOWERS, BIRDS' TAILS AND FEATHERS, AND SCROLLS: Dip brush in water; side-load with S. Blend on palette to soften color and stroke on.

Repeat strokes as in first step, except use Mixture 5.

continued

FULL-SIZE PATTERN

BENCH

Right Center

179

Center of Bench
(see Schematic)

BENCH

Left Center

FULL·SIZE PATTERN

**Butterfly Motif at
Ends of Bench
(see Schematic)**

Bottom Border Design

Top Border Design

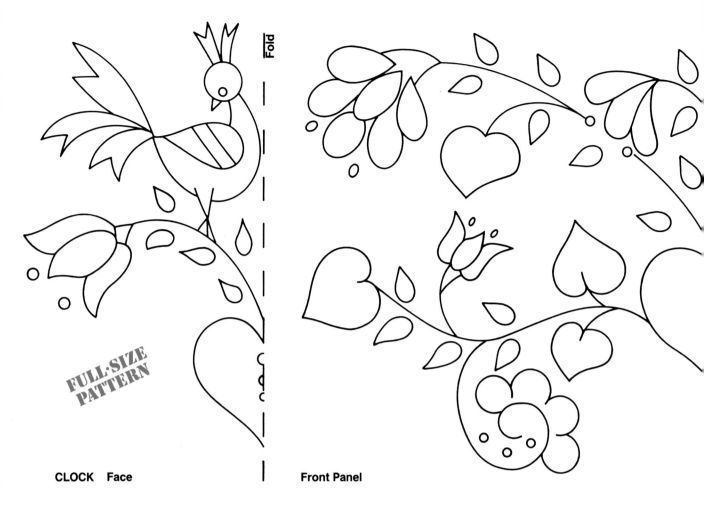

FULL·SIZE PATTERN

Fold

CLOCK Face

Front Panel

YELLOW FLOWER TIPS, SCROLL EDGES, BIRD BODIES, FEATHERS, HEART-SHAPED LEAVES: Dip the brush in water; side-load with YO. Blend on palette to soften color. Stroke around outer edges.

Repeat all strokes as in first step, except use RS.

LEAVES: Dip brush in water; side-load with YO. Blend on palette to soften color. Paint leaf with an "S" stroke starting at the tip.

Next, dip brush in water; side-load with Mixture 3. Blend on palette to soften color, then paint lower half of leaf.

Dip brush into retarder medium; side-load with Mixture 4. Blend on palette to soften color. Stroke on outer bottom edge of leaf.

FINISHING DETAILS: Use the liner brush and thinned BS to paint the outline on flowers, scrolls, hearts, and leaves.

Use the end of the liner brush to add dots of B, YO, and S. Refer to photograph on page 165 for placement details.

ANTIQUING: When painted surface is completely dry, apply a coat of the spray polyurethane varnish. Allow to dry. The varnish facilitates better control of the antiquing. If the antiquing results are unsatisfactory, you can remove the antiquing quickly without damaging the painting.

Mix yellow ocher and raw sienna oil paint in a 2:1 ratio. Blend paint with glazing medium. Dip the large flat oil brush into a mixture of equal amounts of medium and odorless turpentine; dampen the area to be

antiqued from the center outward. Pick up glazing mixture on a brush and start applying glaze to darker areas around the outside of the clock face and front panel. Use less glaze toward the inside surfaces.

Use the soft cloth to wipe off the glaze, beginning in the center. Leave more glaze on the surface toward the outside edge. Soften outer areas using a mop brush. Allow to dry.

VARNISHING: Apply six coats of satin-finish polyurethane spray varnish, waiting 10 minutes between applications. Wait at least 48 hours before applying more of the polyurethane spray. Repeat the varnishing procedure until you have achieved the coverage desired.

Victorian Yard Ornaments

Shown on pages 166 and 167. Approximate finished sizes are as follows: Gentleman, 30x43⅛ inches; lady, 25⅝x40⅝ inches; boy and girl, 20½x26 inches each; baby, 13x20⅝ inches; and dog, 15½x15½ inches

MATERIALS

4x8-foot sheet of hardboard
White latex primer paint
Liquitex acrylic paints in the following colors: Light magenta (LM), naphthol crimson (NC), brilliant yellow (Y), permanent green light (GL), emerald green (G), phthalocyanine green (PG), turquoise green (TG), brilliant blue (B), light blue-violet (BV), permanent light violet (LV), brilliant purple (BP), prism violet (PV), red oxide (RO), raw sienna (RS), burnt umber (BU), Turner's yellow (TY), yellow oxide (YO), white (W), unbleached titanium (T), and mars black (BK)
Assorted round and flat artist's brushes
Paintbrush for primer paint and varnish
Black and brown fine-tip permanent markers
Polyurethane varnish
1x2 lumber (braces)
Paneling adhesive
Hinges (one for each ornament)
Carbon paper
Jigsaw

INSTRUCTIONS

Enlarge the patterns on pages 184–187 onto heavy paper. With carbon paper between the pattern and the board, carefully trace over the pattern outlines to transfer the basic shapes to the hardboard. Arrange the figures to fit on the panel. Cut out the figures with a jigsaw and sand the edges smooth.

PREPARATION: Paint both sides of each cutout figure with two coats of primer. With carbon paper under pattern, transfer detail lines onto the right side of each cutout.

Mix PV and NC to obtain maroon.

GENTLEMAN: Paint the face T. Use RS for hair, mustache, gloves, and boots. Let paint dry, then transfer details of features onto the face. Draw features with brown marker. Paint the eyes BU. Trim boots with BK. Use light strokes with BU to texture the hair.

Paint the tree G with a BU trunk.

Paint the hat BK, leaving the hatband and highlights white. Add the holly in PG and NC berries.

Base-paint the entire coat with maroon mixture; when dry, transfer details. Paint alternating checks of PG and black buttons.

Paint the clown toy's face and hands LM and his suit B. The neck ruffle, pom-pom, and ribbon are Y, and the hair and hat trim are RS.

For the toys, use NC to paint the horn ribbons and alternating stripes on the ball. Paint the horn with TY.

With LV, paint the large scarf flowers, the bow tie, goose's bow, and pant legs. Dot bow tie with BP.

Paint the goose's beak and the man's scarf and vest in Y. When paint is dry, transfer scarf and vest details. Paint details with RO.

With black marker, detail wrist cuffs, shirt, hankie, and goose. Outline and detail each painted area as shown on the pattern.

LADY: Paint the hair TY and the face with T. When dry, transfer face and hair details and draw with brown permanent marker. Fill in mouth with NC and eyes with BV.

Base-paint the dress bodice and skirt TG; when dry, transfer details. Paint some large flowers Y with TY centers and others LV with BP centers. Paint leaves PG and GL. With BV, paint the small flowers and the middle skirt border. When paint is dry, transfer the skirt border detail and fill in the bows with BP.

Base-paint the hat BP; let dry.

Transfer the hat details. Paint the hat bows and bottom skirt border with LV. Finish hat detail with PG holly and berries of NC.

With maroon mixture, paint the large hat ribbons, neck bow, shawl, and remaining skirt border. Leave the fur muff and border trim white.

Transfer the food basket detail to the dry surface. Paint the basket YO, the pineapples and pears Y, and the peaches TY. Fill in cherries and strawberries with NC, the sausages with RO, and grapes with PV. Fill in leaves with G and PG.

Mix a little PG with white to obtain a very pale green to paint the grapefruit.

Detail the basket with the brown permanent marker. With the black marker, detail fur trim and hat ruffles. Outline and detail each painted area as shown on the pattern.

BOY: Base-paint the face and hands T and the hair RS; when dry, transfer facial details. Fill in lips with NC, the eyes with BU, and cheeks LM. Draw details and hair texture with brown permanent marker.

Transfer the shirt detail and paint the hat and pants BV. Use TG to paint the shirt *(except ruffle)* and the hat's brim and stripes. The pant stripes are BP.

Paint the hat pom-pom, neck bow, shirt buttons, pant buttons, and legging stripes with maroon mix.

For the wreath, paint the holly leaves G and the mistletoe TG. Paint the bow and the holly berries NC, leaving the mistletoe berries white. Detail all painted areas with the black marker as for larger figures.

GIRL: Paint face and hair as described for the boy, *above*, making the eyes brilliant blue.

Paint the hat and skirt ruffle BV. When paint is dry, transfer the hat detail. Paint the flower LM.

Base-paint the skirt front LM; allow it to dry, then transfer the detail. With LV, paint alternating skirt checks, hat plume, and dots on the puffy package and pantaloons.

continued

183

VICTORIAN YARD ORNAMENTS

1 Square = 2½ Inches

Paint the cat Y; allow it to dry before transferring details. Paint the cat's bow G. Use G to paint the puffy package bow, hat ribbons, coat, and skirt ribbons. Paint the remaining package bows NC. Add PG holly with NC berries.

Use the maroon mixture to paint the stockings and gloves. With YO, paint the cat's bell and girl's shoes.

Detail the fur trim, wrist ruffle, and all painted areas with the black marker as for the larger figures.

BABY: Use T to paint the baby's face and hands and the doll's face, hands, and legs. Detail the face as for the other children.

Paint the hair Y, adding texture with strokes of TY.

Base-paint the dress pink; let paint dry before transferring details. Paint the dress bows, forearms, and alternating dress stripes with LV, leaving the ruffles white.

Base-paint the doll's dress and hat bow in G; transfer detail when dry. Add Y scallops and leaves.

With BV, paint the doll's bow, forearms, shoes, and dress flowers, and the baby's shoes and remaining dress stripes.

Paint the hair bows maroon and LM. Detail all ruffles and painted areas with the black marker as for the larger figures.

DOG: Base-paint the dog YO and the bow NC. Let paint dry before transferring details.

Paint the collar RO, the bell RS, and the bow stripes G.

Draw the face and all details with a black marker.

FINISHING: Coat all surfaces of each ornament with three coats of polyurethane varnish.

To brace each ornament, cut two pieces of 1x2 lumber to measure ¾ of the ornament's height. Hinge the two pieces together at one short end. Secure one arm of the brace to the back of the ornament with adhesive, positioning the hinge at the top and the open end flush with the base. Open the hinge and lean the ornament back onto the open leg of the brace. *Note:* Making the second leg slightly longer than the one attached to the ornament will enable the figures to stand straighter.

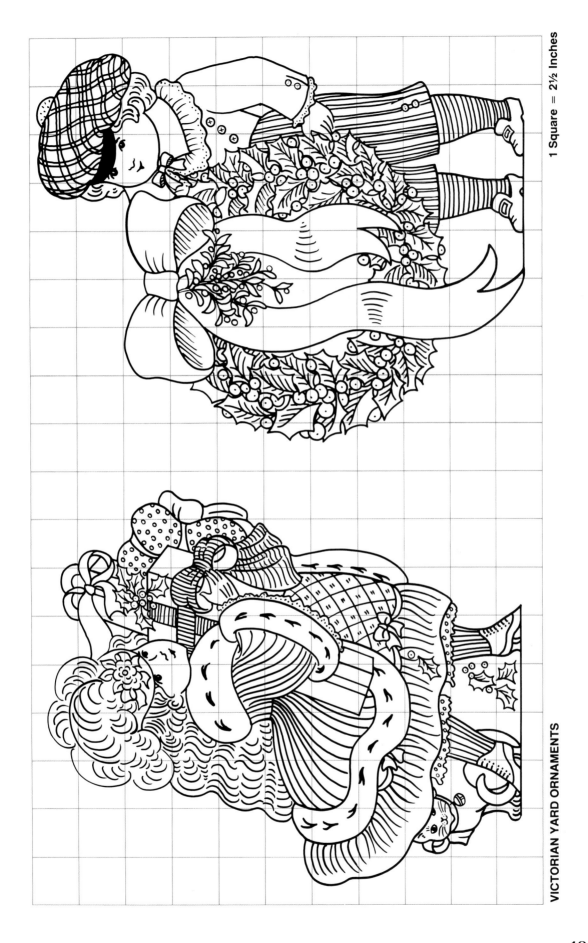

1 Square = 2½ Inches

VICTORIAN YARD ORNAMENTS

185

VICTORIAN YARD ORNAMENTS

1 Square = 2½ Inches

VICTORIAN YARD ORNAMENTS

1 Square = 2½ Inches

187

CREDITS

We would like to express our gratitude and appreciation to the many people who helped us with this book.

Our heartfelt thanks go to each of the artists whose profiles in this book are an inspiration to all those who pursue an interest in the painting craft.

Our special thanks to the designers who contributed projects to this book. When more than one project appears on a page, the acknowledgment specifically cites the project with the page number. A page number alone indicates one designer has contributed all of the project material listed for that page.

We are pleased to acknowledge the photographers whose talents and technical skills contributed much to this book.

For their cooperation and courtesy, we extend a special thanks to the sources who willingly provided us materials and guidance for project development.

And to those talented people whose craftsmanship and technical abilities made it possible to present this material, we also extend a hearty thank you.

Profiles

Ivan Barnett—16–17

Lillian Renko Bledow—18–19

Marie Collette—12–13

Debra Darnall—14–15

John Habercam—10–11

Margaret Miller—8–9

Designers

John Carlton and Dave Wright for Oh Gaude—54, chest

Paddy Crawford—99 and 105, dolls

Carol Dahlstrom—106–107

Linda Emmerson and Janet McCaffery—166–167

Linda Emmerson—56

Kathy Engel—78–83; 100, checkerboard

Jill Fitzhenry—98–99, painted board and chair; 105, chest

Janet Flinchbaugh—48–49, painted board; 54, floorcloth

Becky Franco—38–39; 42–43; 46–47

Meryl Griffiths—161

Petra Haas—49, chest; 50–51; 53

Dana Hall—55

Janet Harrington—57

Joanne Hurley—52, design adaptations

Rebecca Jerdee—21–23; 27

Janet McCaffery and Linda Emmerson—166–167

Margaret Miller—6–7

Nancy Morgan—134–141

Nancy Overton—84

Sally Paul—85; 100–101, sweatshirts

Liz and Peter Robinson—26

Diana Smith—102–103

Rosa Snyder—36–37, painted board; 40–41; 44–45; 158–159, painted board

Tom Thompson—22, stucco wall

Vi Thurmond—159, design adaptation; 160, design adaptation; 162–165, design adaptations

Sara Jane Treinen—20–21, painted board; 37, chest

Jim Williams—24–25; 58–59

Dee Wittmack—108–109

Dave Wright and John Carlton for Oh Gaude—54, chest

Photographers

Susan Gilmore—84–85

Hedrich-Blessing—12–13

Hopkins Associates—6–7, painted
board; 14–15; 20–21, painted
board; 23; 27; 36–37; 40–41;
44–45; 48–49, painted board;
54–55; 78–79, painted board;
98–99; 105; 134–135, painted
board; 158–159, painted board

Michael Jensen—26

Scott Little—19, inset photos; 21,
inset photo; 22; 102–103; 106–107;
166–167

Maris/Semel—10–11; 16–17; 38–39;
42–43; 46–47

Perry Struse—18–19; 24–25; 49,
inset photo; 50–51; 52–53; 56–59;
79, inset photo; 80–83; 100–101;
104; 108–109; 135, inset photo;
136–141; 159, inset photo;
160–165

Jessie Walker Associates—7, inset
photo; 8–9

Acknowledgments

Chroma Acrylics, Inc.
P.O. Box 510
Hainesport, NJ 08036
for Jo Sonja paints for projects
on pages 159, 160, 162–165

Ron Hawbaker

Arlo M. Heggen

Peggy Leonardo

Sue Pennington

Sam and Becky Senti

Don Sires

The Bartley Collection, Ltd.
3 Airpark Drive
Easton, MD 21601
for five-board bench on page 164

Jack West

Don Wipperman

Yield House, Inc.
Route 16
North Conway, NH 03860
for corner display cabinet on
pages 44–45
for Shaker jelly cupboard on
pages 40–41

INDEX

continued